MAKING SENSE OF CRIMINOLOGY

MAKING SENSE OF CRIMINOLOGY

Keith Soothill, Moira Peelo
and Claire Taylor

polity

First published in 2002 by Polity Press in association with Blackwell Publishers Ltd

Editorial office:
Polity Press
65 Bridge Street
Cambridge CB2 1UR, UK

Marketing and production:
Blackwell Publishers Ltd
108 Cowley Road
Oxford OX4 1JF, UK

Published in the USA by
Blackwell Publishers Inc.
350 Main Street
Malden, MA 02148, USA

A catalogue record for this book is available from the British Library.

Library of Congress Cataloging-in-Publication Data

Soothill, Keith.
    Making sense of criminology / Keith Soothill, Moira Peelo, Claire Taylor.
        p. cm.
    Includes bibliographical references and index.
    ISBN 0–7456–2874–5 — ISBN 0–7456–2875–3 (pbk.)
        1. Criminology. 2. Crime. I. Peelo, Moira T. II. Taylor, Claire.
    III. Title.
    HV6025 .S634 2002
    364—dc21

                                                                        2002002150

Typeset in 10.5 on 12pt Sabon
by Graphicraft Limited, Hong Kong
Printed in Great Britain by MPG Books, Bodmin, Cornwall

This book is printed on acid-free paper.

Contents

Boxes, Figures and Tables

BOXES

FIGURES

TABLES

Preface: What is Criminology About?

Many of us might expect criminology to tell us about the amount of crime committed, how much of which crimes occur, who it happens to, who does it, how it is detected, prevented and punished. In short, criminology would be expected to help us answer pressing shared, social problems which arise out of people's illegal and bad behaviours. Crime, after all, often appears to be one of the more straightforward aspects of human activity: on television, in newspapers, among people in general, there is a common expectation that crime is something we should all be able to recognize when we see it, and which we all agree is bad.

So do criminologists provide us with the information to solve these shared problems, or do they make a song and dance about matters of apparent common sense? What *are* the issues that constitute 'common sense'? Is criminology just another academic debate or does it inform us about social reality? Does studying crime contribute to maintaining social order and personal safety, or is it irrelevant to these?

At a personal level, studying criminology requires students to strike a difficult balance between individual, experiential issues and larger, structural questions about how society operates. The impact of crime on victims can be immense; personal fear of crime can adversely influence the quality of many people's lives; and, ultimately, crime can be the malign exercise of power by one person over another. At its simplest, crime is any act that transgresses criminal laws. At a societal level, however, the type of act a society perceives as wrong and proceeds against formally, such as by law, changes over time. *How* wrong we declare an act to be and how sternly we punish it also changes. Who we exclude from legal protection and who we choose to police stringently begs important questions about the nature of society. Perhaps more than many other studies, criminology shows us the diverse and sometimes divided nature of society, rather than always reinforcing the image of a homogeneous, uniform society.

Because society is diverse and varied it can be a hard task for us as individuals to integrate information about personal hurt and grievance with larger questions about society and crime. The latter can seem abstract and irrelevant in the face of the damage harmful acts inflict on people – and harm does not have to be 'major' crime, such as armed robbery; it can be types of vandalism or even litter-spreading. To understand key social issues, additional sorts of information are needed, especially research data, to take us outside our own lives and to inform us about wider patterns. However, we need to be able to evaluate this evidence intelligently, to assess its worth in order to make best use of information – whether to solve particular social problems or to work out how our personal viewpoint fits into a wider social picture.

Criminology, in part, is a debate about ways of assessing and evaluating information to do with crime. As well as informing in straightforward ways about criminals and criminal acts, it provides the tools needed to explore relevant issues in depth; it is, most importantly, a debate about ways of *knowing* about crime and criminals. Hence, as a student, one route to learning to evaluate criminological information is to learn about the debates between criminologists on particular issues. Assessing the worth of information means questioning how and why criminologists construct theory, noting the questions asked and learning to evaluate the methods of data collection and analysis.

To make sense of criminology, then, means recognizing that it is much more than just a set of informed answers to social, criminological problems. Criminology should help us when we grapple, as a society, with balancing personal safety and protection, social order and peace, against notions of social justice, fairness and control in the exercise of power. But to understand criminology one needs to recognize that in the exploration of crime and criminals and in the debate about related social issues, the possible interpretations of apparent evidence represent viewpoints and philosophies which need to be examined along with the evidence gathered.

About this book

This book is an introductory text for new students of criminology. As well as introducing ideas about crime and criminals, it is intended to help new students to make sense of criminology as a *discipline*. At first, it may not be obvious that there is any difference – surely learning about crime and criminals is the same as making sense of criminology? Yet all academic studies come with their own histories and styles of debate, their own questions and structures. We present criminology as a discourse – a particular arena for discussing criminological phenomena. Hence, a new student needs to learn to deconstruct that discourse in order to evaluate the usefulness of information about crime itself.

This book is not a complete account of all you need to know in order to understand criminology. It is selective, picking out key issues, philosophies and debates which will help new students make sense of what criminology is about. It is not an account of every criminological theory, nor is it exhaustively scholastic, summarizing all that every writer – no matter how obscure – has contributed to criminology. We pick key writers and key texts to illuminate the recurring themes and tensions that give criminology its particular character and shape. Criminology is not a straightforward or easy subject, and we make no apologies for presenting sometimes contradictory or conflicting accounts while exploring difficult questions.

Chapter 1 identifies key philosophies in the development of modern criminology, which arises out of the Anglo-American tradition. We discuss its European antecedents, and the major paradigm shift within the Anglo-American tradition that laid down the framework for thinking and research in what is now known as criminology.

Chapter 2 looks at the different ways in which we know about crime – through personal experience, the media (e.g. newspapers, fiction and film), official statistics and research findings. How do criminologists assess and evaluate information?

Chapter 3 is about the criminal justice system – that collection of agencies by which society formally controls deviants. We provide information about different criminal justice agencies, such as the police and the courts, highlighting key tensions in each area.

Chapter 4 considers the concept of justice and questions whether all members of society are treated equally by the justice system. We look at ethnicity, gender and age – all factors which, at some stage, have been explored with concerns about justice in mind.

Chapter 5 outlines some key theories and questions that illustrate important moments in the history of criminological ideas. We ask if it is possible to construct a general theory of crime or if criminologists should try to integrate theories.

Chapter 6 questions how, as an applied subject, criminology links to the public arena of social policy. This chapter illustrates ways of assessing criminology's impact both as 'administrative research' and as 'social commentary'.

Chapter 7 blurs the boundaries of what constitutes crime and criminal behaviour. The difficulty of defining crime is illustrated by exploring three important dilemmas – the policing of the powerful, the policing of protest and the policing of pleasure.

Chapter 8 calls into question what constitutes criminology and highlights the dangers of defining the discipline too narrowly. We consider some of the challenges that lie ahead for the criminology of the future, such as the wider global changes that are taking place.

This book does not give an exhaustive account of everything you need to know to become an expert in criminology. But, by the end, you should have a ground plan which will enable you to go further into the depths, details and complexity of the rich and absorbing study of criminology.

Acknowledgements

Our thanks are too numerous to list, for we need to recognize all those who have been inspirational, engaging, amusing in our quest to understand criminology as well as those who have been amazing in the boldness of their claims. The criminology community has a richness that we hope will continue. This book aims to capture that tradition and to resist attempts to narrow the discipline to a technical exercise.

We hope that we have acknowledged everyone appropriately in the text but oversights sometimes occur. We are struck by Wilson Mizner's adage: 'If you steal from one author, it's plagiarism; if you steal from many, it's research.' Our book espouses research!

One person, the late Barry Sanderson, captures the spirit of this book. Barry came to Lancaster University in the mid-1970s, seconded from the Lancashire Constabulary at a time when there was a dearth of graduates in the police force. He brilliantly weathered the comments in seminars about the supposed inequities of the police. Two vocal Marxist students explained to him that there would be no need for him when there was no class conflict and hence no crime. Barry quietly asked the group: 'Meanwhile, who wants to live in Britain without a police force?' Barry had provided a dose of realism within the academic tower. In the 1980s he completed a doctorate in the management school. After a successful police career, in the mid-1990s he joined a team in the department researching the criminal careers of sex offenders, became a college principal and a lecturer in criminology in the department of sociology. His knowledge, common sense and humour were great assets. His leather gear was a feature of Lancaster corridors. His lectures were much appreciated by students. He was always fascinated by criminology. Sadly, when the research report was being completed, he was killed in a motorbike accident while going for a Sunday 'spin'. He is deeply missed. A close, symbiotic relationship between the academic and the real worlds was what he wanted from the discipline of criminology. We hope that this book captures something of this dream.

Keith Soothill, Moira Peelo, Claire Taylor

The authors and publishers would like to thank the following for permission to use copyrighted material.

Daily Telegraph for box 8.1 (The criminal gene), by Professor Steve Jones, published 27 April 1996, © Telegraph Group Ltd 1996.

The Guardian for box 3.2 (Juliet Bravo), box 4.1 (Justice for all), box 7.1 (Magistrates acquit GM crop protesters) and box 7.2 (Stalking the boundaries), © The Guardian.

The Home Office for permission to use various sections from Home Office publications.

The London Review of Books for box 1.1 (Changing the world), an edited extract from an article by Peter Lipton in *London Review of Books*, 19 July 2001.

Oxford University Press for figure 6.1, 'Tributaries to legislation, 1987–1991' © Lord Windlesham 1993, reprinted from *Responses to Crime, Volume 2: Penal Policy in the Making* by Lord Windlesham (1993).

Sociology Review for box 1.2 (Howard S. Becker, from *Social Studies Review*).

1

Introduction to Criminology

This chapter identifies key philosophies and debates in the development of criminology. Two key schools of thinking – the classical and the positive – arose in Europe and influenced later thinking; but modern criminology arises out of the Anglo-American tradition. A major paradigm shift within the Anglo-American tradition laid down the framework for thinking and research in criminology from the 1960s onwards.

What we are concerned with plotting in this chapter on criminology is what David Garland has called 'a specific genre of discourse and inquiry about crime' (Garland, 1997: 11). We will examine the notion of criminology as a specific kind of discourse by describing some of the key philosophical issues which, at various points in criminology's development, have typified what criminology is or has been.

Current criminology is a study that emerged from a major paradigm shift in the 1960s – and that shift occurred in the Anglo-American tradition. But before the Anglo-American tradition developed and took centre stage in criminology, philosophical thinking in Europe laid down some foundations for that later debate. Strands emerging from the early European debate run throughout criminology, including the Anglo-American tradition. So it is to the contested philosophical roots of criminology that we first turn.

Two scriptural beginnings to the history of criminology

In his entry to *The Social Science Encyclopaedia* Cohen starts off by saying that 'there are two scriptural beginnings to the history of criminology, each marking out a somewhat different fate for the study of crime and its control' (1985: 173). If one can understand the basic differences between these two traditions, then one can understand many of the arguments and debates not only in criminology but also in law, psychiatry and penology. These two traditions are the classical school of the Enlightenment and the positivist revolution of the nineteenth century.

Cohen argues that the beginning dates from the mid-eighteenth century and is the outcome of the work of Enlightenment thinkers like Beccaria (1738–94) and Bentham (1748–1832) in breaking with what can be identified as a previously 'archaic', 'barbaric', 'repressive' or 'arbitrary' system of criminal law. This was the *classical school*. For these reformers, the crime question was predominantly the punishment question. Their programme was to prevent punishment from being, in Beccaria's words, 'an act of violence of one or many against a private citizen'; instead, it should be essentially 'public, prompt, necessary, the least possible in given circumstances, proportionate to the crime, dictated by laws'. Classicism presented a model of rationality, with a limited liberal state imposing the fair and just punishment that must result if social harm has been perpetrated.

Almost a century after classicism, criminology was to claim for itself another beginning and another set of influences. This was the positivist revolution and popularly dates from the publication in 1876 of Lombroso's (1836–1909) *L'Uomo delinquente*. The new positivist programme was to focus not on the *crime*, but on the *criminal*; it did not assume rationality, free will and choice (typical concepts within the classical debate); instead, determinism – with biological, psychological or social constraints – challenged the notion of individual choice. This new tradition began to identify the criminal as a special person or a member of a special class. The underlying aim of this new criminological agenda was to produce a general causal theory by which to explain criminality. This quest gave the subject its distinctive and collective self-definition – 'the scientific study of the causes of crime'.

These two philosophical positions – often known as the classical and positivist standpoints – are usually set out as two totally separate traditions. The classical tradition was superseded by the positivistic approach by the end of the nineteenth century and then made a dramatic comeback in a slightly revised form from the early 1970s onwards. While it may be easier to read history in these stark terms, it does not match reality. Judges, for example, have always had to juggle with the claims of lawyers – usually working within a more classicist tradition and insisting on free will and responsibility. Psychiatrists, on the other hand, tend to work within a positivist tradition, insisting on a more deterministic stance with internal and external factors compromising notions of free will. It has always been so.

There are few 'pure' classicists and few 'pure' positivists. Most of us, in fact, embrace notions from both traditions. However, some criminologists lean more in one direction than the other. These two traditions manifest themselves in three approaches that appear and reappear throughout the study of criminology:

- A *legal approach* emphasizes the classical tradition and notions of free will.
- A *biological approach* emphasizes the positivist tradition and links with psychological approaches.
- A *social approach* originally the positivist tradition – but with a major paradigm shift in the 1960s. There are considerable theoretical variations within this approach.

These three distinct strands currently co-exist and have run through the history of criminology. Sometimes they interweave, sometimes they conflict, and the spotlight shines brightly on one or more at given times. These philosophical underpinnings and their tensions need to be remembered as we now turn to consider some of the key moments and debates in the development of criminology.

The development of criminology

This book does not provide a traditional history of criminology, but criminologists from Britain and the United States of America tend to get very possessive when they talk about the development of criminology. As we consider the emerging battlefield for criminology we need to remember that the early skirmishes were fought on the continent of Europe – certainly not in the United States of America, where criminology had not yet secured a place, not in Britain, which took a rather detached view from things happening on the mainland of Europe.

Anyone averse to history can skip the next section without too much harm. However, it sometimes helps to know a bit of background when the current development of criminology suggests that history may be repeated. Overall, what we recognize as modern criminology arises out of the Anglo-American tradition (hence we give it most space); yet its roots lay in Europe. What follows are key moments that define and highlight important developments in criminology, grouped under three main headings:

- remember Europe;
- Anglo-American tradition;
- so where are we now?

Remember Europe

Few now recognize the importance of early European thinking for the new study of criminology. While it is still debated whether or not such thinking constitutes criminology as we now know it, these ideas provide an early introduction to systematic thinking about criminal justice and punishment. Certainly, theorizing about crime and punishment loomed larger in France (and on the Continent generally) in the nineteenth century. This points to an interesting distinction between mainland Europe and the Anglo-Saxon countries. The latter – and here we are talking about Britain and the United States of America – tend to attack their problems by pragmatic experimentation. Indeed, Gordon Wright has suggested that 'the history of crime-control efforts in Britain or the United States can probably be written without much reference to theoretical disputes (though not without reference to mores and values)' (1983: 110). In contrast, in France theorizing about crime is taken seriously and has evolved over time.

The classicists argued that excessive and brutal punishments were unworthy of civilized nations. They stressed that the essential purpose of punishment was utilitarian rather than vengeful: each penalty should be precisely calculated so that the pain imposed would just outweigh the pleasure of successful wrongdoing. A pure form of utilitarianism would have little use for the notion of retribution – often spoken of as the Old Testament's 'eye for an eye and tooth for a tooth' justice. However, while the utilitarian views of Jeremy Bentham were particularly influential in Britain, Beccaria and his French followers mixed their utilitarianism with a continuing element of retributionism, and this mixture of the two elements emerged in the thinking of the 1789 revolutionaries and in Napoleon's penal codes.

Hence, in France it was a particular blend of utilitarianism and retributionism that eventually came to be known as 'classical' theory (Wright, 1983). The sharp edges of classical theory soon began to be softened somewhat in France: the revision of the penal code in 1832 reflected this by authorizing judges and juries to reduce charges and penalties on the basis of extenuating circumstances. The advocates of change later came to be called the neoclassical school, combining utility and retribution in thinking about suitable punishments. Throughout the rest of the nineteenth century, the neoclassical school was to dominate criminological theory in France, and it retains a strong influence among jurists and penal authorities down to the present day. The challenge to the neoclassical doctrine began to emerge in the mid-nineteenth century and then, more concretely, in the form of the so-called positive school of criminology.

Important medical influences also had a relevance to the eventual growth of criminology. For example, Dr Philippe Pinel advanced the theory of 'moral insanity' as an explanation of some criminal behaviour and suggested that some criminals should be treated, not punished.

More importantly, the work of Dr Benedict Morel had great impact in the mid-nineteenth century when he put forward the concept of degeneracy (Pick, 1989). Both crime and madness, wrote Morel, were growing in epidemic fashion. In his terms they were traceable to a process of moral and physical decay, brought on among the working classes by disease, unwholesome living quarters, alcohol, drugs and adulterated foods; the consequent degeneracy was transmitted to the children and grew progressively worse (Morel, 1857). However, he recognized that criminals were different from insane persons; as they still had a choice, they should not be treated for a form of illness. Degeneracy theory had an immediate and lasting impact. It was widely accepted by the public, and by writers on crime, until well into the twentieth century.

The intense discussion in France in the third quarter of the nineteenth century was interrupted by the publication in Italy of Lombroso's startling book *L'Uomo delinquente* (1876), which forced them to grapple with his unorthodox theory. Lombroso (1835–1909) was a young army doctor who based his initial work on a study of army recruits. He claimed to have identified a category of 'born criminals', who were characterized by certain physical characteristics.

These included: an under- or over-sized brain, a receding forehead, high cheekbones, squinting eyes, bushy eyebrows, a twisted nose and big ears. (As late as the 1930s, judges were ordering Lombrosian analyses of defendants' physiques.) Lombroso's work, based on what seemed to be scientific observation, was a forthright manifesto of the new positivistic spirit.

Few books in the history of criminological theory have caused such a stir. Importantly, his work seemed to harmonize with the new scientific spirit of the age and appeared to open up a clearly marked path to the control of crime. The prevention of crime became a reasonable goal, for if potential criminals could be so accurately identified, then their crimes might be averted by surveillance or internment. It suddenly made the idea of punishment seem outmoded. If offenders were predestined to a life of crime, it would be meaningless to talk of punishment; the new alternatives would either be curative treatment or elimination of the criminal for the good of society.

In fact, the work of Morel and some other French doctors had already anticipated Lombroso's position in their theories of moral insanity, degeneracy and the inheritance of pathological tendencies. While those of the classical tradition were appalled at what they regarded as the new heresy, Wright explains how the French scene became more complex. In brief, the counter-attack was led not so much by those in the classical and neoclassical tradition, but rather by a group of French positivists who mobilized in opposition to the Italian positivists and, in turn, developed a rival French school of positivism that shifted the central emphasis from biological to social factors and so edged out the 'pure' Lombrosians from the centre of the stage.

While few would have known it at the time, this ideological battle between the Italian and French positivists became equivalent to a criminological Olympic Games, with the French and Italians pitted against each other for world supremacy. The initial encounter in this contest came in 1885, when the Italians convened the first international Congress of Criminal Anthropology in Rome. The new congress produced controversy and not a harmonious new orthodoxy. Dr Alexandre Lacassagne, a professor of legal medicine from Lyon, challenged the basic assumptions of the Lombroso school and charged that its practical consequences would be devastating; it would leave societies, he said, with no choice but to keep all deviants locked up in prisons or asylums. Lacassagne then put forward the basic premise of what was to emerge as the rival French school of criminal sociology, namely that crime was mainly the product of social causes. At the end of his address he said that 'societies have the criminals they deserve'.

In these early controversies in Rome we can see the three important approaches to studying crime and criminals that we have already mentioned: a legal approach; a biological approach; a social approach.

Such controversy did not destroy the development of criminology but it influenced its subsequent profile by laying down its 'fault lines' – the fissures along which dispute erupts. In fact, current criminology is a study that emerged from a major paradigm shift in the 1960s – and that shift occurred in the Anglo-American tradition. So, to make sense of that shift we need now to examine the development of criminology in Britain and in the United States of America.

Anglo-American tradition

Britain and early criminology

David Garland's broad historical argument is that the social and intellectual rationale for modern criminology grew out of the convergence of two quite separate enterprises: what he calls 'the governmental project' and 'the Lombrosian project'. Garland's use of the term 'project' is important to grasp: he uses it 'to characterize an emergent tradition of inquiry which, despite a degree of variation, shares a cluster of aims and objectives' (1997: 12). The 'governmental' project refers to those inquiries that direct attention to the problems of *governing* crime and criminals. Studies within this tradition need not necessarily be official, state-sponsored studies but, certainly from the nineteenth century onwards, the state has come to dominate work of this kind. The 'Lombrosian' project, on the other hand, refers to that tradition of inquiry, begun by Lombroso, which aims to differentiate the criminal individual from the non-criminal.

Garland's main argument is that the discipline continues to be structured by the sometimes competing, sometimes converging claims of these two programmes. So, of the two poles, there is one which pulls towards an ambitious (and according to Garland deeply flawed) theoretical project that seeks to build a science of causes. The other exerts the pull of a more pragmatic, policy-orientated, administrative project, seeking to use science in the service of management and control. It is the latter strand that was firmly established in Britain from the late 1950 onwards. However, we need to establish what happened in Britain before this point. What was the British reaction to the gladiatorial contests between France and Italy in the late nineteenth century in relation to the embryonic science of criminology?

In fact, the attitude of Britain was rather like England's tepid attitude to the early football World Cups, in which it simply failed to participate. The 1896 Geneva Congress of Criminal Anthropology was the first occasion when Britain sent an official delegate – the prison inspector Major Arthur Griffiths – and Griffiths came back to file a rather sceptical report of developments on the Continent.

There were individual enthusiasts of Continental ideas in Britain, such as Havelock Ellis and William Douglas Morrison, and possible early precursors of Lombroso, such as the psychiatrist Henry Maudsley and the prison medical officer J. Bruce Thomson, but the official British position was one of a certain detachment. Generally, prison doctors and experienced psychiatrists recognized that the majority of criminals were more or less normal individuals and that only a minority required psychiatric treatment, which usually involved removing them from the penal system and putting them into institutions for the mentally ill or defective. Most of the major scientific works on crime written in Britain before the 1930s were by doctors with psychiatric training and positions within the prison service. The most significant was the work of Dr Charles Goring, *The English Convict: A Statistical Study*, published in 1913, which was essentially a challenge to Lombroso's claims. *The English Convict* had a considerable impact abroad, and especially in the USA, but in Britain it received a much more muted response. However, Goring's approach is important, for it inaugurated a new stream of statistical studies that has strongly influenced criminological work, especially in the post-war period in work done and commissioned by the Home Office.

Certainly Garland suggests that 'scientific research on individual criminals in Britain stemmed from a rather different root than did continental criminology, and inclined towards a more pragmatic institutionalised approach to its subject' (1997: 37).

However, as the positivist movement on the Continent became less extreme in its claims – influenced largely by the emerging French tradition – and indeed more pragmatic, the initial hostility of Britain's scientific and penological circles tended to fade.

Focusing on the research, writing and teaching in criminology that did take place up to the Second World War, Garland makes the useful point that it all came close to the concerns of the Lombrosian project in its focus on individuals and their differential classification.

But what needs to be recognized is that the British work essentially lacked the scientific ambition and theory-building of the Lombrosian project, being almost exclusively concerned with knowledge that was useful for administrative purposes.

Garland identifies Maurice Hamblin Smith as Britain's first authorized teacher of 'criminology' and as the first individual to use the title of 'criminologist'. Hamblin Smith was intensely interested in psychoanalysis, both to assess the personality of offenders and as a technique for treating the mental conflicts which, he claimed, lay behind the criminal act.

In the early 1930s there was sufficient interest in criminological matters in England to develop the Association for the Scientific Treatment of Criminals (1931) which, in 1932, became the Institute for the Scientific Treatment of Delinquency (ISTD). Most of those involved in this initiative were in private clinic work – at the Tavistock (1921), the Maudsley (1923), the new child guidance clinics and, in 1933, the ISTD's own Psychopathic Clinic (which in 1937 was moved and renamed as the Portman Clinic). As Garland stresses, this new field of practice gave rise to its own distinctive brand of criminological theory with an interest in the clinical exploration of the individual personality.

Another strand of British criminology prior to the Second World War can be identified and represented by the eclectic, multifactorial, social-psychological research of Cyril Burt. Interestingly, when later criminologists such as Radzinowicz and Mannheim look back upon the work of their predecessors, Garland notes that they do not talk of Charles Goring or Hamblin Smith; they focus on Burt's 1925 study, *The Young Delinquent*, as the first major work of modern British criminology. So Radzinowicz states (1961: 173–6): 'it may be said that modern criminological research in England dates only from Sir Cyril Burt's study of *The Young Delinquent*, first published in 1925. Its excellence in method and interpretation was at once recognised and it has stood the test of rapidly advancing knowledge' – a fascinating statement in the light of subsequent doubts, expressed shortly after Burt's death, that he fudged his figures!

Garland sums up by emphasizing quite correctly that 'the scientific criminology which developed in Britain between the 1890s and the Second World War was thus heavily dominated by a medico-psychological approach, focused upon the individual offender and tied into a correctionalist penal-welfare policy' (1997: 44). In contrast, influence from *sociological* work – such as that developed from the insights of Durkheim in France at the turn of the century or from the Chicago School, the influential group of sociologists from the United States in the inter-war years – was non-existent.

So up to the Second World War (1939–45) British criminology responded to problems which were thrown up by the system – by the courts, the prison and the Borstal system – such as mentally abnormal offenders, recidivists and especially juvenile delinquents. As Garland so eloquently emphasizes, 'the central purpose of scientific research [that is, in Britain at least] was not the construction of explanatory theory but instead the more immediate end of aiding the policy-making process' (1997: 44). In other words, in Garland's terms, the 'governmental project' dominated in a narrowly defined way. This is not surprising as the researchers and teachers on criminology prior to the Second World War were largely practitioners working in prisons, clinics or hospitals. Criminology as a university-based, academic discipline simply did not exist.

The domination of American criminology

The situation was very different in the United States. Studying crime and deviance within a university setting became firmly entrenched well before the Second World War. The development of the University of Chicago sociology department was crucial. This department was constituted in 1892, but it began to become important in the study of crime and deviance when Robert Park, an ex-journalist, became its head.

Chicago sociology ranged widely in its work. As Downes and Rock point out, 'it was not the express ambition of the Chicago sociologists to focus on crime and deviance' (1998: 69); furthermore, criminology was not treated as a separate sub-discipline. The concern was a more general one – seeking solutions to *social problems*. 'Social problems' was the title of the relevant course in many American university departments – more familiarly known to generations of American students as 'nuts and sluts' courses.

The approaches of Chicago sociologists were diverse – as Downes and Rock have commented: 'The Chicago sociologists had no binding commitment to the discovery of any single explanation or any single *kind* of explanation' (1998: 76). Their strengths were as empirical sociologists (i.e. collected data as evidence), using a variety of methods – personal documents, anthropological fieldwork, the analysis of census and court records – to probe contemporary crime and deviance.

As interest in crime and deviance began to develop in Britain in the 1950s, ideas from America and the Chicago School started to percolate. Terence Morris's pioneering study, *The Criminal Area* (1958), was a replication of the ecological approach developed in Chicago in the 1920s and 1930s. Downes and Rock suggest that 'there seemed to be an affinity between the turbulent and expanding Chicago of the 1920s and the cities of England in the 1960s and 1970s' (1998: 81).

Influenced by theoretical and empirical work from the USA, particularly Chicago, crime began to be studied in much more earnest in Britain in the late 1950s and early 1960s, but the main development came with the massive expansion of the undergraduate teaching of sociology in the 1960s and early 1970s. In Britain criminology was becoming a postgraduate qualification. Two developments in the funding and organization of research took place in London and Cambridge in the late 1950s and was crucial to the subsequent development of criminology.

The development of 'administrative criminology' in Britain

Since the Criminal Justice Act 1948 the Home Secretary had been given power to spend money on research into criminological and penal matters, but a total of only £12,000 was spent in the next decade. Hence, Rab Butler has explained how, by the time he became Home Secretary early in 1957, 'the mood of Parliament and the country favoured a radical reappraisal of the penal system' (1974: 1). In May 1957 Butler announced the formation of the Home Office Research Unit, which at that time consisted of two research workers and four civil servants, and in June 1957 he was encouraged by the Howard League for Penal Reform to give support to a proposal to establish an Institute of Criminology by approaching the vice-chancellors of the universities. In July 1958 Butler announced to Parliament that Cambridge would establish the Institute if sufficient funds could be made available. Leon Radzinowicz became the first Wolfson professor and director in the summer of 1959. Butler states: 'In general the announcement of the Institute's establishment was well received with features and leading articles in the major newspapers, but in some quarters the response was lukewarm.' (1974: 8).

This coolness on the part of the academic criminologists and sociologists continued throughout the 1960s. It was a time of massive developments in the sociology of deviance, and there was a willingness to question and challenge the more traditional approaches to criminology that were evident in the work of the Institute of Criminology at Cambridge and the Home Office Research Unit in London. Many sociologists of deviance became unhappy at the close links, perhaps more apparent than real, between the Institute at Cambridge and the Home Office in London.

John Martin, who worked at Cambridge in the 1960s, has reminisced: 'Ironically it was the function of giving of advice to government which never developed as an Institute activity, although Radzinowicz himself was a member of the Home Secretary's advisory council. The rest of the staff was too heavily engaged to have the time to offer advice on an intermittent basis even if asked' (1988: 174). Perhaps the Institute never really kept the close contacts with the Home Office which other academics suspected; however, it certainly lost contact with the mainstream developments in social science within universities. Martin reflects: 'Some of us said at the time, the Institute in its early days was a centre of criminological research but not of criminological thought' (1988: 173).

A paradigm shift

Meanwhile, criminological thought was becoming embroiled in a major debate within sociology that erupted in the 1960s and had its origins in some concerns about the most appropriate way to study crime and deviance. Its effect on criminology was to become most recognizable in the 1970s.

This shift in the mid-1960s both in Britain and, more importantly, in the USA arose as a challenge to the assumptions of a positivist model of thinking (called a 'paradigm shift', following the work of Thomas Kuhn – see box 1.1). Within criminology it is most often associated with the name and work of Howard Becker, but other important figures were also influenced by what became generally known as the labelling approach. The intellectual parentage of this approach was in the work of G. H. Mead in the 1930s relating to 'symbolic interactionism'.

However, it was certainly Howard Becker (see box 1.2) with his famous book, *Outsiders* (1963) who captured the mood of the moment so successfully. It is understandable that this book attracted attention for it was well written and its main focus was the interesting topic of marijuana smoking and the notion of becoming deviant. What was happening was the growth and development of a specifically *sociological* view of deviant phenomena, and many of the insights

BOX 1.1   CHANGING THE WORLD

At a New York cocktail party shortly after the Second World War, a young physics postgraduate blurted out to a woman he had met there: 'I just want to know what Truth is!' This was Thomas Kuhn. Soon afterwards he gave up physics for the history of science. The work that followed, especially *The Structure of Scientific Revolutions*, published in 1962 and now with sales of well over a million copies, was the most important contribution to the history and philosophy of science of the twentieth century.

Kuhn was struck by the consensus among those working in particular disciplines during periods of what he came to call 'normal science'. It isn't just that they accept the same theories and data, they also have a shared conception of how to proceed in their research, a tacit agreement of where to look next. There is agreement about which new problems to tackle, what techniques to try and what count as good solutions. It is rather as if new practitioners in a particular discipline are covertly given copies of a book of rules, the secret guide to research in their field.

What he found was that scientists learn to proceed by example rather than by rule. They are guided by what Kuhn called their *exemplars*, or certain shared solutions to problems in their speciality. Scientists will choose new problems that seem similar to the exemplary ones, will deploy techniques similar to those that worked in the exemplars, and will judge their success by the standards the exemplars exemplify.

Exemplars also create their own destruction, as they will eventually suggest problems that are not soluble by the exemplary techniques. This leads to a state of crisis and in some cases to a scientific revolution, where new exemplars replace the old ones and another period of normal science begins. This whole process is known as a paradigmatic shift. Kant claimed that, after a scientific revolution, 'the world changes'.

Source: Adapted from 'Kant on wheels' by Peter Lipton, *London Review of Books,* 19 July 2001, pp. 30–1

BOX 1.2   HOWARD S. BECKER

Becker's writings on the sociology of crime and deviance sparked considerable excitement and controversy in the 1960s. Their challenge lay in statements on the nature and importance for sociologists of partisanship and moral commitment – Becker's work is often described as a 'sociology of the underdog' – and in their rejection of the narrow, individualist explanations of traditional, positivist criminologies. The labelling approach to understanding deviance, an approach to which Becker's name is most closely linked, emphasizes deviance as a social process, a product of the interaction between the 'offender' and the wider social audience.

In his book *Outsiders*, first published in 1963, Becker outlined his basic position on deviance, saying that it 'is not a quality of the act that the person commits, but rather a consequence of the application by others of rules and sanctions to an "offender". The deviant is one to whom the label has been successfully applied; deviant behaviour is behaviour that people so label' (1963: 9).

These lines helped to fan a fierce debate inside and outside academic circles about the social construction of deviance and about social policy for dealing with deviant behaviour.

Source: Adapted from the article 'Howard S. Becker', *Social Studies Review*, November 1987, pp. 75–6

---

captured by this approach were then imported into mainstream criminology.

In his important book *Becoming Deviant* (1969) Matza identified three major phases in deviance work, which were developing concurrently rather than consecutively:

1   appreciation of the deviant;
2   human pathology being replaced by diversity;
3   the erosion of the divide between deviant and conventional.

We now focus on these phases to identify and explore the major paradigm shift that was occurring.

1 *Appreciation of the deviant* First of all, Matza identified the replacement of a correctional stance by an *appreciation* of the deviant subject. Roughly, the correctional view, at least from the standpoint of the sociologist, is that bad things result from bad conditions. Hence, the aim is to eradicate or correct those bad conditions, and from this follows the implication that there will be no more bad things. Certainly, in its original form, the correctional view did not entertain the possibility of evil arising from things deemed good – and vice versa. In fact, this was a contribution of the much-maligned functionalist school – associated mainly with Talcott Parsons – that many things deemed bad had latent functions that were good.

Matza felt that one of the basic difficulties with the correctional perspective is that it systematically interferes with the capacity to empathize and so really comprehend the subject of inquiry. By contrast, appreciative sentiments mean that we do not want to rid ourselves of deviant phenomena. Instead, we are intrigued by them.

These sentiments are regarded as an intrinsic, vital part of human society. In other words, we want to 'appreciate' the deviant's own account. Equally, though, we should not regard the deviant's account as the only story. For while the correctional stance may be inappropriate for a sociological approach, equally dangerous is the other end of the pendulum – the trap of romanticizing deviance. To appreciate is simply to estimate justly the deviant's own account.

Closely associated with 'appreciation' is the concern to defend a conception of deviance as meaningful action. Stan Cohen's example is vandalism (1971). Vandalism, unlike the property crime of theft, cannot be explained in terms of the easily understood motive of acquiring material gain, for the property is damaged, not revered. As a consequence, it is easily described as motiveless. One interest, then, was in restoring meaning to behaviour that could be so easily described as 'meaningless', 'senseless' or 'irrational'. The argument was that doctors – and, in particular, psychiatrists – were much to blame for annihilating much of the meaning of deviant and criminal behaviour by writing off the person as 'sick' rather than recognizing that the people participate in *meaningful* activity.

2 *Human pathology replaced by diversity* This brings us indirectly to Matza's second phase in the growth of a sociological view of deviant phenomena, namely the purging of a conception of pathology – that is, crime as a disease – by a new stress placed on human diversity. The idea of pathology has a long history. By the time of the

Chicago School there was ample evidence to reject an account of *personal* pathology, but the concept of pathology was quickly located at the *social* level in so far as social disorganization became the operative idea.

The most well-known questioning of social pathology is contained in the work of Goffman. What is considered pathological by those in white coats in a mental institution may seem normal enough in the client's subculture. Those administering the wards have a vested interest in order and in a career and may be motivated to regard behaviour that is troublesome to those running the ward as a symptom of the client's illness. Goffman opens up the world of the double-bind situation: if the patient says the food tastes like soap, he is crazy; if he says the food is OK, then he also must be crazy. In fact, the striking thing about Goffman's work is that he takes particularly bizarre human conduct and is still able to question the capacity to impute pathology.

3 Erosion of the deviant-conventional distinction   The third aspect which Matza identified in the growth of the sociological view of deviant behaviour is the gradual erosion of the simple distinction between deviant and conventional phenomena. The gradual elimination of the simple distinction between the conventional world, on the one hand, and the deviant world, on the other, leads to a more sophisticated view stressing *complexity*.

Both implicit and explicit in this sociological view of deviant phenomena was an attack on positivism. Matza (in his earlier – and more influential – book *Delinquency and Drift*, 1964) summarized what he saw as the fatal legacy of positivist criminology against which the new paradigm was constructed. The three underlying assumptions he picked out had developed, he argued, in reaction – or rather, overreaction – to the assumptions of classical criminology associated in particular with Beccaria and Bentham. Matza regards the three fundamental assumptions underpinning positivist criminology to be:

- a stress on the importance of the criminal actor rather than on the law;
- a stress by the positivists on the quest for scientific status;
- the notion of the constrained delinquent.

So the positivist school explains crime by the motivational and behavioural systems of criminals. Hence, as a contribution to understanding crime and deviance, the law and its administration are deemed simply secondary at best or totally irrelevant at worst.

Matza draws attention to the classic debate between the classical school and positivism: 'whereas the classical school accepted the doctrine of free will, the positive school based the study of criminal behaviour on scientific determinism' (Jeffrey, 1960: 379; cited in Matza, 1964: 5). In brief, it was suggested that the quest for scientific respectability resulted in some damaging philosophical assumptions being made. Matza maintained that positivists rejected the view that man exercized freedom, was possessed of reason and was thus capable of choice. For the positivist, the delinquent was fundamentally different from the law-abiding person.

Post-paradigm shift

So where did this paradigm shift take the study of criminology? The increasing focus on and appreciation of the deviant's account (and the rejection of the correctionalist stance), the recognition of the diversity and complexity of the situation made what was becoming mainstream criminology less attractive for government sponsors of research. In turn, some academics felt that they were supping with the devil if they accepted research commissioned by government. So, for around two decades, the split between much academic criminology and mainstream policy-making was perhaps greater than has been generally recognized.

With the rising popularity of sociology in the 1960s, a new generation of graduates found the medico-legal emphasis of much of British criminology very limited and limiting. The National Deviancy Conferences held at York in the late 1960s symbolized a deliberate break with what was seen as the stranglehold on the subject by the orthodox criminology of the south-east, represented by Cambridge and the Home Office. The collections *Images of Deviance* (edited by Stan Cohen, 1971) and *Politics and Deviance* (edited by Ian Taylor and Laurie Taylor, 1973) include a range of examples of this new work, mostly placed within the context of the sociology of deviance. Cohen and Taylor's book *Psychological Survival* (1972) produced a stir for several reasons. The study was on the experience of imprisonment under maximum security conditions in H Wing at Durham Prison. Cohen and Taylor published their work in defiance of the provisions of the Official Secrets Act governing research into penal and allied establishments and was a stand against even liberal forms of censorship.

There was a flood of publications in the deviance area in the 1970s. However, Downes usefully highlights the developing tensions within the National Deviancy Conferences, which eventually fissured or split in 1973. Downes suggests that 'the politics of the NDC pivoted around the tensions between those who primarily sought intellectual as distinct from those who emphasised political radicalism' (1988: 178). Downes correctly identifies how criminology was beginning to fragment in the 1970s or, more elegantly put, 'by 1974, several competing theoretical approaches were on offer' (p. 178). From the late 1970s to the present day criminological work has been conducted with a lower level of theoretical intensity but with a greater attentiveness to policy as well as to political issues.

Certainly the development of a Marxist, critical or radical criminology, particularly identified with the publication of *The New Criminology* (Taylor and Taylor, 1973) and of *Critical Criminology* (Taylor et al., 1975) attempted to continue to move the mainstream of criminology away from the administrative centres of power. However, while very influential in a variety of ways, one needs to recognize that Marxist approaches were never mainstream criminology. In contrast, some of the insights loosely associated with the interactionist or labelling perspective were taken on board more broadly in the increasing fragmentation of criminology in the 1970s and early 1980s.

So where are we now?

Since the 1960s some of the assumptions underpinning mainstream or conventional criminology have shifted quite dramatically. Having said that, there is a dispute about what can be regarded as 'mainstream' or 'conventional' criminology. What is undoubtedly true is that the psychiatric and psychological approaches were increasingly taking the back seat, although both these disciplines were themselves experiencing changes. Certainly the dominant theme of the first half of the twentieth century – that of the criminal being conceptualized as a particular type of person, understandable and, where it is considered appropriate, treatable apart from society – had been successfully challenged.

Of course, there are periodic flurries that still feed this old tradition. So, for example, in the early 1970s there was the discovery of chromosomal abnormalities among patients at special hospitals, such as Broadmoor and Rampton. In fact, there is a small proportion of these patients who have committed (or were alleged to have committed, for many of their cases did not go to trial) some very bizarre crimes and for whom a chromosome abnormality has been detected. However, such numbers would certainly have very little impact on the major questions of crime causation. The crucial point to remember is that offenders are not fundamentally different, in this sort of way, from the rest of us.

Criminology is more complicated than such a simple divide between offenders and the rest of the world allows. Since the 1970s the discourse of criminology has become more fragmented, extending its reach to allow detailed examination of its conceptual base. Important issues and concepts such as race and gender, whose meanings and impact may in the past have been assumed, became themselves the focus for study and exploration. Hence, theoretical vantage points (e.g. Marxist, feminist, Marxist-feminist) became both more fundamental and more varied. At the same time, crime became a key social and political concern which demands practical answers and applications from researchers. New Left Realism (which we look at in more detail in chapter 5) was one major response to this cocktail of pressures shaping criminological debate, and it looked for practical outcomes to crime problems in combination with theoretical exploration. Crime has become a central concern in election campaigns and in newspaper and television reporting; hence there is continuing pressure to recognize and prioritize the practical outcomes of research and how they relate to the problem of crime control.

Conclusion

This chapter is not a traditional history of criminology; instead it has identified key debates to illustrate important shifts in thinking within the criminological discourse over time. Underpinning these debates are assumptions about the purposes and uses of criminology. We have suggested two different sets of beginnings to criminology (both arising from Europe):

- the classical school;
- nineteenth-century positivism.

Modern criminology, while it draws on those roots, is more usually understood as the result of the major paradigm shift of the 1960s within the Anglo-American tradition. However, not all commentators have been moved by the paradigm shift, and it is noteworthy that some of the earliest ideas informing criminology remain influential today. For example, Gottfredson and Hirschi (1990) draw on insights from the classical tradition in outlining their theory of self-control (which is discussed further in chapter 5).

Criminology is still seen as a relatively new study, indeed many still regard criminology as an infant that cannot stand on its own feet. However, we have seen that criminology has a longer history than is sometimes realized. It is always difficult to identify a beginning to a subject that has always been talked about; people will always have held a view – a theory – as to why some steal and others do not. In 1721 Daniel Defoe in his novel *Moll Flanders*, would not have been the first to say words to the effect, 'Give me not poverty lest I steal'. The greater likelihood of someone stealing if they are in poverty is not a modern insight and does not need the discipline of criminology to suggest it. Which of such discussions does one declare to be the beginning of a specialist study?

Perhaps one of the ways of recognizing the arrival of an autonomous subject comes when the discourse becomes typified by tension and rebellion. Certainly there was tension and rebellion in the 1960s in plenty – civil unrest in the USA, student rebellion in Britain and a clearer link between student and worker concerns in continental Europe. Most particularly, there was dissension within the ranks of sociologists. Over the years criminology has certainly strengthened its claim to exist as an autonomous, multidisciplinary subject but, as Stan Cohen argues, 'somewhat like a parasite, criminology attached itself to its host subjects (notably law, psychology, psychiatry, and sociology) and drew from them methods, theories and academic credibility' (1988: 2). However, most subjects have done the same in drawing away from parent disciplines. Anyway, unlike many 'bastards' whose parentage is not always claimed, with criminology there are several parents – as well as grandparents – of this infant that need to be recognized.

Rather than concerning ourselves too much with the semantics of the words 'discipline', 'field of study' or even 'field study', we have presented criminology here as a discourse because this best represents the idea that there are processes of reasoning which underpin criminological knowledge. The reasoning and arguments implicit in the dialogues described in this chapter have something to say about what constitutes knowledge in criminology and how we should interpret it. And it is to the subject of 'information' that we turn in chapter 2: what do we know about crime and how do we know it?

2

Knowing about Crime

There are different ways in which we know about crime – through personal experience, media (e.g. newspapers, fiction and film), official statistics and research findings. They can all contribute to our knowledge of crime and to the ways in which society frames criminological problems and solutions.

Crime is a compelling subject, a matter of popular interest and focus for much press, television and cinema activity. Most of us have images of crime, a sense of the story of crime, criminals and detection – yet rarely through direct experience alone. Few of us could, for example, describe precisely where our pictures of police and policing have come from. Popular awareness and understanding of police work owes much to fiction and television or cinema portrayals as well as to personal experience or knowledge.

Murder, in particular, has become a major topic for novels and television drama, as has also the heroic figure of the detective and the drama centred on police activity. *Dixon of Dock Green*, *Z Cars* and *The Sweeney* were just a handful of the original television dramas that were set in police stations and purported to represent the reality of police work. They set the scene for what we recognize as police drama today: the car chases, the radios and other paraphernalia of police technology, the lone detective set against the camaraderie of uniformed officers. How do students of criminology begin to assess what are inherited images, drawn for their entertainment value, and what is 'real' knowledge about police work?

This strange relationship between fiction (designed to satisfy popular interest) and police work has existed for some time: George Scott-Moncrieff compiled *The Casebook of a Victorian Detective* out of two volumes of McLevy's account of his time as a member of the Edinburgh Police Force between 1830 and 1860 (McLevy, 1975). McLevy first worked for the Edinburgh Police Force as a night watchman, only later becoming a detective. He was greatly proud of his deductive capacities, which were not presented as the product of superior intellect but as an outcome of his awareness of small matters – noting something out of place or seeing a known criminal behaving suspiciously. His manner of observing the human drama – to walk through but not to be a part of, to reflect and to observe, to don disguise or to hide in wait and to carry out surveillance – acts as a precursor to all the stratagems that later characters of fiction, such as Arthur Conan Doyle's heroic detective, Sherlock Holmes, have taught us to expect in police behaviour. Indeed, Scott-Moncrieff speculated that Conan Doyle might easily have read McLevy's stories when a student in Edinburgh.

Dixon of Dock Green is, of course, one of the best known of the early television police dramas: often popularly assumed to represent a real historical time of innocence, when bobbies walked the beat and when crime was supposedly less violent and less common. Dixon himself is sometimes used to represent the reality of the honest, upright copper who exercises wise discretion in the course of his duty. What is less well known is that in the film which predated the television series, *The Blue Lamp* (1950), Constable Dixon is shot dead halfway through. The film portrayed car chases and the police use of modern technology (especially radio), along with a squad of heavy-smoking detectives skilled in deduction, evidence gathering, surveillance and the organization of operations. The soldiery on the beat were respectful of their superior, officer class and found time to practise the police choir's rendition of 'nymphs and shepherds' in between reliefs.

The Dixon view, then, shows police responding to crime as and when it happens. There is little complexity about whether or not criminal activity is policed more among certain sectors of the population than others. Indeed, *real* crime is presented as an almost private activity, conducted by professional criminals of the 'old school' according to a particular set of rules, and policed by a fair-minded bunch of coppers who knew the game. Indeed, the threat to this private arrangement is shown to come from out-of-control, violent youth who do not play by the rules.

Whether or not such a comfortable view of policing is the only version of reality is arguable. Sir Robert Mark, Commissioner of the Metropolitan Police from 1972 until 1977, began his life as a policeman in 1937 in Manchester. While his early experience represented the world of the regular bobby on a regular beat in the manner we have come to associate with Dixonesque policing, Mark described it in less cosy terms than we are used to, both in respect of the public and of the police themselves: 'There was no suggestion of leadership by example. Seniors battened on and bullied juniors and the force as a whole did the same to that part of the public not able effectively to look after itself' (1978: 20). As well as recognizing that the force could be neglectful and careless (p. 31) he also commented that 'there was a willingness by the police to use violence against the hardened criminal' (p. 52), a willingness which he felt had become increasingly rare over time.

So, already we have two conflicting, alternative accounts of policing, one before and one after the Second World War. How do we begin to assess which is right and which is wrong, or how, in their different ways, both pictures inform us of aspects of early policing? How do we begin to evaluate which picture helps us to better understand crime and the police responses to it? The legacy we have inherited, with its familiar images of detection and policing, was present in the earliest television and cinema dramas, as well as in the longer-established medium of the printed word. But familiar images are not always accurate ones, and historically well-established accounts sometimes need updating. As the gulf between Mark's biographical account and the television portrayal of Dixon illustrates, there can exist a gap between representation and reality in our understanding of policing, crime and criminals.

Fiction can feel as if it muddies the waters. Yet the cheerful cockneys who appeared in *The Blue Lamp* are frequently extras in our communal history of crime. A common belief about life during the Second World War was that the whole population 'pulled together' without complaint. This shorthand description of the past assumes a golden age in which everyone could trust their neighbours and all children were loved and well-disciplined. Hylton examined a range of material from official statistics to Mass Observation reports, and challenges this rosy picture of wartime behaviour. In reality, the reported crimes 'rose from their 1939 level of 303,711 (England and Wales) to 478,394 in 1945, and the number of people convicted was similarly up, by 54 per cent' (2001: 153). The crime scene changed, with fewer motoring offences and less drunkenness but with more looting, theft and profiteering, black marketeering and hoarding. The Home Office were concerned about juvenile crime and truancy, and Hylton reports that 'eighty thousand schoolchildren were running wild in London by the end of 1940' (2001: 165).

Learning to make sense of criminology starts with acknowledging that we all make assumptions about crime, criminology and the justice system. As we have seen with the Dixon history of policing and Sir Robert Mark's view, conflicting accounts exist concerning the same phenomena. To make sense of criminology, then, we need to recognize that there are different types of knowledge operating and informing our understanding of crime. Two types which we have encountered in these historical examples are:

- direct experience of crime;
- mediated experience.

Direct experience of crime can be as victims, as criminals, as neighbours, as relatives, as onlookers and as workers in the justice system (e.g. in the police, courts or Probation Service). Mediated experience, by contrast, tends to come to us indirectly via press, radio, TV, cinema or fiction.

Further types of information emerge from the example of crime during the Blitz in the Second World War:

- official information;
- research knowledge.

These are the types of knowledge which, generally, are beyond our personal experience, and while communications media – such as newspapers, television and the Internet – use official information and research knowledge to fill space on the news pages and time on our television screens, their coverage of such sources is very limited.

All four types of knowledge – personal experience, mediated knowledge, official information and research knowledge – contribute to how we know about crime. Interestingly, however, all such knowledge is partial. In other words, each one of us might experience some aspect of crime; the media tend to interpret data in stereotypical ways; official statistics, by definition, only include information known to officials; while research knowledge is limited in scope and tends to concentrate on specific matters of concern.

To begin to unravel and explore some of these issues about knowledge we will now focus on the official story of crime and later move on to consider how we might learn more from other sources.

The official story of crime

Where do we find official statistics?

There has been a remarkable shift in the availability of official information since the arrival of the Internet. Instead of being largely reliant on their college or local library for gaining access to official documents, students can now find many publications on-line. Of course, the official information is limited. Much information is either still not available on the Internet or not available in any form.

Here we are concerned with the ordinary 'bookkeeping' criminal statistics, based on data drawn from parts of the criminal justice system, such as the police, the courts or the prisons. In Britain, regular and systematic compilations began only in the early nineteenth century; now *Criminal Statistics: England and Wales* are published routinely each year. The general census, first established in 1801, provides scope to relate the figures on crime to those of the general population. Other useful publications that appear annually include *Prison Statistics: England and Wales*; *Report of Her Majesty's Chief Inspector of Constabulary* and *Report of the Commissioner of Police of the Metropolis*.

Beyond these annual publications, there are other one-off sources published by the government, many of which are now available on-line. So, for example, the command paper, *Criminal Justice: The Way Ahead* (Home Office, 2001), of which hard copies could be purchased through retail outlets at £15.70, can now be viewed and printed out free via the Internet. The Home Office disseminates research findings and relevant statistics through the Research Development Statistics website: http://www.homeoffice.gov.uk/rds/.

What do official statistics tell us?

Official statistics tell us which actions, reports and decisions within the justice system have been formally recorded. Hence, while official sources are important, they can mask as much as they reveal about crime. Prior to the 1960s, criminologists, failing to recognize the dangers, often based their theories on 'facts' from official statistics.

Within a traditional framework, it was thought there was not much wrong with official statistics which could not be put right by more careful recording. However, after the 1960s it was more difficult to make this claim as there were critics ready to remind us what the official statistics actually say.

The obvious point is that statistics are the tales told by officials, for that is what makes them 'official'. However, Kitsuse and Cicourel (1963) went beyond this obvious point by focusing on the processes of crime rate construction. The official rates of crime are produced according to *the actions actually taken by persons in the social system*, actions that define, classify and record certain behaviour as a crime. For example, if the police are very active, then there will appear to be more crime – even though the actual amount of criminal behaviour may remain the same. In other words, crime rates may be a better measure of the activity of the organizations producing the statistics than of the actual amount of crime.

So what's the current story of crime? The following figures are taken from Annex E of *Criminal Justice: The Way Ahead* (Home Office, 2001). Typically, nearly 14,500 notifiable offences will be recorded by the police *on any given day*. Notifiable offences are recorded offences that the police are required to notify to the Home Office. Of these, around 14 per cent will be crimes of violence, 58 per cent burglary and thefts, 3 per cent drug offences and less than 1 per cent will be sexual offences.

In addition to the notifiable offences, the police deal with large numbers of other offences, the largest group being motoring offences. Typically, just over 12,500 motoring offences will be dealt with *each day* by one of several possible processes (e.g. issuing a fixed penalty notice or a report for summons).

Understanding criminal statistics

Deconstructing what official statistics are telling us requires clarity about how figures are collected at different stages in the criminal justice process as well as clarity about what statistics mean. To understand official data collection in more depth, we will look at the 'recording' of statistics and the problems this can present to the police; and then at 'attrition' to show the filtering process that occurs in the justice system.

Recording – police   As we saw above, the scale of work that directly involves the police each day is breathtaking, and the problems of policing are complex. Certainly, the demands are increasing and this sometimes involves the collecting of statistics. A report *On the Record* (Povey, 2000) by the inspectorate of constabulary concluded that hundreds of thousands of offences, including assaults, burglaries and car crimes, were excluded from national statistics because of police inefficiency and bureaucracy. The report called for a national system of recording to try to eliminate inconsistencies between forces in the way crimes were recorded. The concern was that too many decisions on whether a crime had taken place were left to individual officers.

The recommendation was that victims should confirm the nature of the crimes. A Home Office spokesman claimed: 'This will be a more victim-centred approach and will lead to increased clarity and transparency' (*Guardian*, 12 July 2001). He also conceded: 'This will inevitably lead to an increase in crime figures, because it will include a larger number of low level crimes which might previously have been omitted from police recorded crime statistics.' This admission led to the headline, 'New system means official crime figures may rise by 20%'. It is planned to introduce the new system of recording offences in all 43 police forces in England and Wales in 2002.

Attrition in the criminal justice system   This section is adapted from Annex A 'Attrition in the criminal justice system' (Home Office, 2001). 'Attrition' is the term used to describe the filtering process that occurs between a crime being committed and the person who committed it being sanctioned by the police or courts. Only a small proportion of those committing a crime reach the final point of an appearance in the courts. One can think of it like the Grand National horse race in which horses fall at various hurdles on the way to the finish. What is a major problem for the police and, ultimately, the public is that fewer horses now reach the finishing point.

Comparing statistics over time is always hazardous, and the task is to ensure that shifts in counting procedures have not undermined the argument being proposed here. One can say with some confidence that the clear-up rate has fallen and the conviction rate is declining.

Figure 2.1 compares attrition in 1980 and 1999–2000. The total number of *recorded* crimes in each year is set to 100 per cent. It needs to be noted that we are talking here about *recorded* crime – that is, crime that comes to the notice of the police and gets recorded – and not about all crime that is committed. Once a crime has been recorded by the police, the first hurdle to confront is whether the offence is cleared up or not. As figure 2.1 shows, the clear-up rate has

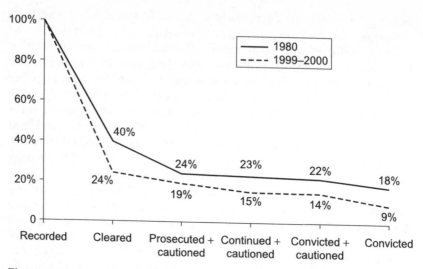

Figure 2.1 Attrition after the point of recording: 1980 and 1999–2000
Source: 'Annex A: Attrition in the criminal justice system', *Criminal Justice: The Way Ahead* (London: HMSO, 2001)

fallen from 40 per cent in 1980 to 24 per cent in 1999–2000. This seems quite serious – and, indeed, it is. As we have seen, such a fall could mask differences of procedure.

The next stage shows the percentage of persons prosecuted or cautioned in 1980 and in 1999–2000. Twenty-four per cent of the former and 19 per cent of the latter reached this point. While there is much current concern about the low clear-up rate, one can see from figure 2.1 that a major issue in 1980 was the loss of cases between clear-up (40%) and prosecution and caution (24%).

After the point of prosecution or caution, one can see that the curve is much flatter for both 1980 and 1999–2000. In other words, the percentage of cases being 'lost' at each hurdle is much lower. The next stage considers the percentage of persons who are cautioned or whose case proceeds to a court hearing (i.e. excluding cases terminated early) and shows that the gap between the two years has widened again. Moving on to the percentage of persons convicted or cautioned one can see that the same gap has been maintained. Finally, consideration of the percentage of persons convicted shows that the gap has marginally widened. Perhaps more important, figure 2.1 shows that the proportion of cases that reached conviction halved between 1980 and 1999–2000 – 18 per cent in 1980 and only 9 per cent twenty years later.

So what do we make of it all? What can we say with some confidence? It is certainly the case that over the last twenty years, the number of crimes *recorded* has increased considerably – the Home Office estimates that the increase is over 70 per cent on a like-for-like counting basis. This is partly due to the increased reporting of crime. There has also been a suggestion that, over time, more of the incidents reported by victims have been recorded by the police as crimes.

The Home Office (2001) makes some provisos about the calculations, stressing that figure 2.1 should only be seen as a *guide* to how the performance of the system has changed over the last twenty years. So, for example, the types of offences covered by the two series are not identical – more offences have come on to the statute book – and there have been changes in data quality and procedures over the time period shown. The Home Office points out that one notable change was the revision to the counting rules used by the police for recording crime, which was introduced in April 1998. It is also stressed that the comparison is between *crimes* recorded and cleared up and *persons* dealt with by the criminal justice system for indictable offences. There is not a precise match between the two and many people confuse the two when they look up the *Criminal Statistics*. Some offenders appearing in court are often dealt with for more than one offence (including offences taken into consideration). It is these issues of reading and interpreting statistics to which we now turn our attention.

Interpreting statistical data

Using and understanding criminal statistics is much more demanding than is sometimes recognized. Being a criminologist requires learning how to read criminal statistics properly. We will unravel two common problems that are experienced in interpreting criminal statistics:

- the dangers of confusing offences and offenders;
- confusing daily and yearly averages in the prison population.

Confusing offences and offenders

The *Criminal Statistics: England and Wales* largely focus on offenders rather than offences, although one would perhaps not realize this from a quick read of the pages. The main presentations are divided between indictable and non-indictable offences. 'Indictable only' offences are the most serious breaches of the criminal law and must be tried at the crown court. 'Indictable only' offences include murder, manslaughter, rape and robbery. Summary offences, on the other hand, are those triable only by a magistrates' court. These are mainly motoring offences but also include such offences as common assault and criminal damage up to £5,000. If an offender is convicted of both an indictable *and* a non-indictable offence, there is an entry in both of the sections. However, if, say, an offender is convicted of two indictable offences, then only the *principal* offence is included in the *Criminal Statistics: England and Wales*.

This all sounds rather technical. Does it really make any difference? In trying to understand crime, it may. For instance, if a person is convicted in court of twelve counts of burglary, he (and it is usually a 'he') will appear only once in the *Criminal Statistics* – for the burglary offence for which he got the longest sentence. However, in terms of the police statistics – 'crimes known to the police' – each of the burglaries is likely to have been recorded separately. Sometimes there seems to be a massive discrepancy between the crimes recorded by the police and the numbers appearing in the *Criminal Statistics*. This will be for two reasons – one a fact and one an artefact.

- There is a massive filtering process going on. Crimes known to the police only comparatively rarely last the full distance to the conviction and sentence of a perpetrator. Earlier, we suggested it is like the Grand National race with many fallers (see 'Attrition in the criminal justice system').
- The artefact sometimes makes the difference appear even greater than it actually is. Police statistics tend to focus on offences while the *Criminal Statistics* are about offenders.

Another quirk of the *Criminal Statistics* is that one cannot really tell how many persons were, for instance, convicted of rape last year. If John Smith is convicted for both burglary and rape and the judge decides that the burglary is the more serious offence and sentences accordingly, then the rape conviction will not appear as such in the *Criminal Statistics*. Probably the most important use of the *Criminal Statistics* is comparative: for instance, how many persons were convicted of rape this year compared with last year? If a similar proportion of rape convictions are masked in this way each year, then this shortcoming does not totally undermine the comparison.

Confusing daily and yearly averages in the prison population

There is much discussion about the prison population. Sometimes we are told how many prisoners are held in prison on a particular day (i.e. on a census day) and sometimes we are told how many prisoners have been imprisoned during the course of a whole year. These two sets of figures provide quite different results. Many more will have been imprisoned during the course of the year than are in prison on any one day. This suggests two major problems in comparing these two sets of figures:

- The number of prisoners held on a particular day will emphasize the number of persons sentenced for a longer term.
- The yearly figures will emphasize the number of persons sentenced for shorter periods.

An example may help. There are two cells in prison. One cell is occupied by a long-sentence prisoner who stays there for a whole year. The second cell is occupied by a series of short-sentence prisoners – each month one is released and replaced by another. On a prison census day there will be one long-sentence prisoner in cell one and a short-sentence prisoner in cell two. If this is the pattern throughout all the prisons, then the result would be that half the prisoners in the prison system are short-term prisoners and half the prisoners are long-term prisoners. (A researcher might conclude that 50 per cent of prisoners are long-term prisoners and 50 per cent are short-term.)

In contrast, taking the year as a whole, there will be one long-sentence prisoner in cell one and twelve short-sentence prisoners in cell two over the course of the year. If this was the pattern throughout all the prisons, then the result would be that 8 per cent (that is, one out of thirteen prisoners) are long-term prisoners and 92 per cent are short-term prisoners. This is a very different picture to the one portrayed by a census, when it seemed that half of the prison population were long term.

Unknown crime

We have seen that official statistics reflect activity within the justice system, and do so in complex ways. A criminologist needs an eye for detail, and awareness both of how the justice system works and how to interpret evidence. In addition, one needs to acknowledge that

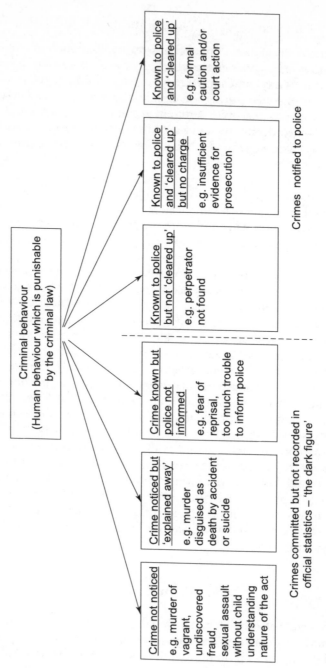

Criminal behaviour
(Human behaviour which is punishable
by the criminal law)

Crime not noticed

e.g. murder of vagrant, undiscovered fraud, sexual assault without child understanding nature of the act

Crime noticed but 'explained away'

e.g. murder disguised as death by accident or suicide

Crime known but police not informed

e.g. fear of reprisal, too much trouble to inform police

Known to police but not 'cleared up'

e.g. perpetrator not found

Known to police and 'cleared up' but no charge

e.g. insufficient evidence for prosecution

Known to police and 'cleared up'

e.g. formal caution and/or court action

Crimes committed but not recorded in official statistics – 'the dark figure'

Crimes notified to police

Figure 2.2 Interpretation of official criminal statistics

official statistics necessarily limit discussion because they cannot encompass crime that is unknown to the system. Moreover, the concept
of 'unknown crime' leads to the possibility that the experience of
victimization may not be reflected in records of offences or offenders.

Far more crimes are committed than ever come to police notice:
for example, the crime may be victimless and pass undetected, or a
victim may decide not to report a crime. Figure 2.2 shows various
outcomes following behaviour which, in theory at least, is punishable
by the criminal law. The big divide is between:

- crimes committed but not recorded in official statistics ('the dark
  figure');
- crimes that are notified to the police.

Figure 2.2 gives three examples of crimes that are committed but
not recorded: a crime may simply not be noticed (for example, a sexual
offence may be perpetrated on a child but the child does not understand the nature of the act); the criminal activity may be noticed but
is 'explained away' (for example, a murder may be successfully disguised as an accident or suicide); the crime may be known about but
the police are not informed (for example, there may be a fear of
reprisal if a crime is reported).

Even if a crime is notified to the police, there can be various outcomes. Figure 2.2 identifies three possibilities: a crime may be known
to the police but they cannot find the perpetrator, so it is not 'cleared
up'; a crime may be known and is 'cleared up', but there can be no
charge as there is insufficient evidence for prosecution; finally, a crime
may be known and 'cleared up' *and* some formal action may be
taken. In the latter outcome the case may get to court but there may
be an acquittal. In such circumstances the police may still regard the
case as 'cleared up' – in a domestic violence case, for instance, the
court may acquit even though there is no other possible perpetrator –
or the case may remain open if there is a chance that the wrong
person had been charged.

Victims

By now it will be clear that it is not known how many crimes are
committed every day and that far more crimes are committed than
ever come to police notice. Ignorance is the mother of research, and a

major initiative of the Home Office in the 1980s was to begin to probe this conundrum. The resulting British Crime Survey (BCS) has become a vital tool in attempting to assess levels of victimization by moving outside the confines of traditionally gathered official statistics.

Using methods largely developed in the United States of America, this massive task was well orchestrated by Pat Mayhew and her colleagues at the Home Office. While there have been criticisms in terms of both the technique used and some of the interpretations of the results, the work has generally been widely applauded. In fact, there has been both consistency (so that results of one survey can be compared with the next) and refinement (so that the surveys are steadily improving). In addition, over the years there have been additional one-off questions (that is, questions for a particular survey). In brief, however, the basic idea involved in conducting a victim survey is to ask questions couched in everyday language rather in legal terms, for example: 'in the last . . . months, has anyone got into your house without permission in order to steal something'?

The British Crime Survey provides estimates for only certain categories of crime. These crimes are robbery, theft from the person, household theft, vehicle-related thefts, vandalism, common assault, wounding and burglary. The BCS was first started in 1982 and is now conducted annually. There are some crimes that can never be 'captured' by the BCS, for some hazards for the community do not figure in the criminal statistics but are potentially much more serious and widespread in their effects: environmental pollution, health and safety in factories and even unethical business practices may be much more crucial to the survival and well-being of the community than many of the criminal issues highlighted by the media and politicians. However, it is difficult to find such activities recorded in *Criminal Statistics*, and those who design victimization surveys usually fail to consider such problems. More importantly, though – and this illustrates a major drawback of victimization surveys – what happens if people are not even aware that they are victims? For example, environmental pollution may be affecting everyone, but if no one notices there will be no record. To do something about crime, one must know that it exists (Abercrombie et al., 2000: 531).

The figures from the BCS suggest that around 40,000 of the offences included in the survey are committed *each day*, and of these 39 per cent are reported. Interestingly, if we take those categories of crime covered by the BCS that can be directly compared with police categories, we can identify that around 55 per cent are recorded.

However, there are difficulties with national surveys. Jock Young and his colleagues (Jones et al., 1986; Painter et al., 1989) argued that local surveys enable us to move beyond the abstraction of aggregate national statistics. As Young points out, 'crime is extremely geographically focused and policing varies widely between the suburbs and inner city'. In combining these very different geographical areas to produce national figures, he suggests we distort what life is really like for those living in some parts of the inner city. Young notes that the first British Crime Survey suggested that 'the "average" citizen would suffer a robbery once every five centuries; burglary once every 40 years; and assault resulting in injury (even slight) once every century' (Young, 1991: 103). Hence, for the 'average' citizen it may be an irrational fear to get seriously worried about most crime. But Young's point is that fears become highly rational for certain groups, particularly those living in certain city areas.

We can already begin to see to what extent crime and criminality cannot be understood by examining only officially recorded crimes, offences and offenders or, indeed, numbers of prisoners. Even within the relatively clear-cut parameters of the British Crime Survey, viewing life from a 'victim' vantage point completely alters perceptions of the levels of criminal interaction and experience within society.

Research: meanings, vantage points and methods

Research

So what can 'research' do that is not already done by official statistics (or, indeed, by personal experience and mediated accounts)? The word 'research' is used quite loosely here; one must not assume that only academics in universities carry out research beyond the compilation of official statistics. Research, in its widest sense, can allow wide-ranging questioning and the exploration of apparently clear-cut issues, teasing out what underpins contradictions and looking for depth in explanations of crime.

So, for example, the 'British' Crime Survey relates only to England and Wales, and the Scottish Executive (formerly the Scottish Office) conduct their own crime survey, the Scottish Crime Survey. There seem to be important differences between these two jurisdictions. Soothill and Francis (2002) have discussed how – using data from the crime surveys – Scotland seems to have lower violence rates than

England and Wales. Data from other sources shows that Scotland has a higher homicide rate than England and Wales (Soothill et al., 1999). Trying to understand why England and Wales have a higher violence rate but a lower homicide rate than Scotland is the sort of puzzle that criminologists try to grapple with.

Research is characterized by the generation of data in order to explore identified questions and issues. It is typified by systematic gathering and the analysis of data from a variety of sources and by a variety of research methods. The range of methods used (from surveys based on stratified samples to qualitative interviews) are shared with official statisticians and researchers who, as we have seen with the development of the British Crime Survey, do indeed engage in research activity beyond the generation of official data alone. The purposes in gathering official statistics, however, relate to a need to manage social order and the agencies of the justice system. While criminological research may contribute to these social goals, it also has more freedom to question in depth what constitutes information, how data is managed and interpreted, and what it tells us about criminological phenomena. Where official statistics *describe*, research *investigates*.

At one level, research is most easily understood as a systematic attempt to build on previous knowledge by gathering and examining evidence which helps us to further clarify particular social phenomena, in this case evidence related to crime and criminal activity. There is tension between the systematic nature of research and its focus, phenomena that are concerned with the complexity of human action and the fluidity of social change. Similarly, the categories of 'crime' and 'criminal' are not unproblematic. How does one explore or reconcile the perceptions of varied groups or explain the social meanings of their standpoints? What meanings do we ascribe to differing perceptions and who assumes the authority to interpret and define meaning?

Meanings

Official statistics tend to work within the 'given parameters' of the crime debate. So, for example, they tend not to problematize what constitutes crime and what meanings given crimes have for society. For example, Becker's account of marijuana use, mentioned in chapter 1, raised questions about the margins of criminality. Rather than assuming law-breaking to be one, uniform activity, a criminologist might want to explore some of the complex meanings surrounding particular behaviour, some of which is criminalized and some of which is not.

Even with the most serious crimes, each act is not seen as equally bad or interpreted in precisely the same way. Murder is a case in point. It is one of our most serious offences, carrying heavy penalties and social disapproval. In terms of maintaining an ordered and orderly society, most of us would wish the state to ensure that our right to continue living is protected. The impact of sudden, often violent, but certainly untimely death on friends, relatives and acquaintances of the victim is one of deep and shattering disturbance.

Yet the judgements made about murder and murderers are situational and focus on supposed intent. In other words, society does not really believe murder to be wholly wrong on every occasion; every illegal killing is not always defined as murder. How can this be so? One way to distinguish levels of social disapproval is through the language chosen to describe an action. What is popularly called murder is, in reality, 'homicide', an umbrella term which covers a variety of killings. Mitchell dedicates the first chapter of his book on *Murder and Penal Policy* (1990) to taking us in detail through the complications of the words homicide, manslaughter and murder, as well as to discussing other illegal deaths, for example, infanticide, or causing death by reckless driving. He invokes Sir Edward Coke's definition of murder as: malice aforethought bringing about death within a year and a day of an inflicted hurt (p. 3). The apparent casuistry of the debate about which actions are murder and which are not can sound legalistic. Yet murder is viewed as one of our worst of crimes, and Mitchell concludes that retaining a distinction between manslaughter and murder 'allows the stigma of murder to be maintained and recognises the variations that exist between one unlawful killing and another' (p. 37). The definitions, then, help us to express the appropriate level of social disapproval. For criminologists, as well as for the courts, the variety of actions that happen under the headings 'murder' or 'homicide' might require a range of explanations.

Vantage points

Whose perspective, then, do criminologists represent? Whose views should researchers explore? One approach to evaluating the worth of research knowledge is to question from whose vantage point the work is written – not to reinforce the old, cynical view that everyone has an axe to grind, but rather to establish where the vantage point is and whether this is of use to you. The vantage point might be that of an observer, attempting to give relatively equal weight to the views of all participants. It might be trying to establish the experience of victims or the motivation of offenders. Different research designs give rise to different sorts of knowledge – perhaps descriptive, perhaps experiential. How researchers choose to analyse their data tells the reader about the questions being addressed and what is recognized as real knowledge in that project. Where researchers are positioned in relation to the subject of study will often be reflected in the choice of research methods, such as participant–observer or social statistician.

Researchers recognize that vantage point matters when investigating crime. As we have seen, inherent in victim surveys is a move from defining crime through formal agencies alone, to the notion of crime as an experience whose definitions do not depend solely on the workings of the justice system. Research usually encompasses these wider visualizations of crime and criminality and, further, recognizes that there may be competing systems of morality underpinning legal and illegal acts. So, for example, in an ethnographic study Janet Foster (1990) explores attitudes to petty crime and the law within families in one locality. From this vantage point, petty offending can be seen as a kind of conformity within that milieu. Criminological research can inform us about the social dimensions and meanings of law-building and law-breaking. What does this tell us about a society's beliefs about right and wrong?

Research methods

As we saw in chapter 1 with regard to positivism, it is also true that embedded within the choice of research methods are assumptions about what constitutes knowledge. (Ferri and Lombroso represented the idea that crime must be studied as a *science*, with all that this implies about procedures, knowledge and interpretation.) Such assumptions inform the researcher's *methodology* – that is, the philosophy that steers and shapes their research questions, research methods and beliefs about what can constitute knowledge in criminology. However, such philosophies are not always made explicit. Indeed, it is often assumed that the choice of methods automatically indicates that a piece of research must represent a particular stance – without questioning any further. Choice of methods may be used as a short-hand to indicate that the underlying philosophical debates have been dealt with.

The main divide is between quantitative and qualitative data collection. A common mistake is to assume that anything with numbers means positivism, while anything with interview material represents qualitative research. It is, however, perfectly possible to analyse interviews in ways that reduce all experiential information to a form of head-counting, and not all statistical work necessarily imitates a nineteenth-century view of the physical sciences in conduct or philosophy. Intent in a research project (what it is trying to achieve) and vantage point are key considerations in choice of method, as well as the researcher's philosophy about what constitutes evidence and knowledge.

Qualitative research methods were a part of the Chicago School revolution. Interviewing respondents and participant observation became essential in exploring vantage points from *within*, rather than offering only an outside commentary of a phenomenon (see box 2.1). The voices of respondents as diverse as those in deviancy studies (Matza, 1969) and in studies of women within the justice system (Carlen, 1985) have only been heard through such methods. We have already seen some of the problems attached to interpreting descriptive statistics, and qualitative methods bring their own characteristic difficulties of collection and analysis – not least, how the researcher positions their vantage point and commentary in relation to respondents' reflections and lives.

Framing criminological questions

We started this chapter by suggesting that each individual holds assumptions about crime and criminals that are drawn from a variety of personal and mediated sources. Starting to make sense of criminology requires each of us to be prepared to question our assumptions and where they have come from, and to be aware of how different types of knowledge contribute differently to our overall picture of what constitutes reasonable knowledge about crime. The complexity that emerges from questioning and evaluating what is known and how it has become known can be frustrating, even disorientating. Crime is, however, an important social issue: fear of crime shapes people's lives; much money and time is spent attempting to solve

---

BOX 2.1   PARTICIPANT OBSERVATION: ETHICAL ISSUES

In his classic study observing a street-corner gang in Boston, William Foote Whyte noted: 'As I sat and listened, I learned the answers to questions that I would not have had the sense to ask if I had been getting my information solely on an interviewing basis' (1955: 305).

In *Street Corner Society* (1955) Whyte discusses the experience of being a social anthropologist and a participant–observer in one's own society. At the heart of his study was a wish to avoid the tendency 'to look upon communities in terms of social problems so that the community as an organized social system simply did not exist' (p. 286). Some ethical and practical problems he highlighted for participant observation were:

- making false starts and finding the right people to make the work possible;
- living in the area throughout the project;
- explanations;
- conflict between complete immersion in the district and personal honesty;
- making contact some time later and receiving feedback on published work.

Source: W. F. Whyte, *Street Corner Society*, 2nd edn (Chicago: University of Chicago Press, 1955)

---

problems related to crime. At the very least, criminologists must evaluate evidence effectively, to assess what we *really* know and how useful information might be.

How we go about solving criminological problems as a society does not depend on the discourse of criminology alone. In this chapter we have distinguished between four types of knowledge about crime:

- personal experience;
- mediated experience;
- official statistics;
- research knowledge.

Yet, in reality, we know that these types of knowledge are unlikely to work independently of each other; they are more likely to interact. There is a fifth type of knowledge at the disposal of students of crime that moves beyond the collection of empirical data, and that is scholarship. By examining material in detail (whether it be criminological theory, research findings, official statistics or the development of policy) one builds a picture of crime; perhaps, as important, one can take a step back and engage in a commentary on the *debate* about crime.

Few societies find total agreement about the definitions of dangers within their midst. How a criminological problem is framed – then addressed or solved – and what the underlying evidence is may not always match. Indeed, Thompson (1998) has argued that since the 1960s we have been subject to a rapidly changing succession of what he describes as 'moral panics', in which perceived threats to social order have led to pressure on politicians and society to take action. Thompson argues that there is a spiralling interaction of media, public opinion, special interest groups and authorities which encourages moral panics (around, for example, child killings or paedophilia or, in earlier time, teddy boys and youth behaviour). In times of social change there is room for conflict over what constitutes morality and acceptable values. This increases

> potential for value conflicts and lifestyle clashes between diverse social groups, which turn to moral enterprise to defend or assert their values against those of other groups. They do this within a public arena which offers many media outlets for amplifying their fears and articulating demands for social control and regulation to defend those values. (Thompson, 1998: 11)

Hence, formulating criminological questions and finding solutions to society's crime problems is the concern of many groups, some working inside the justice system and some having little to do directly with the workings of the law. Criminologists are but one set of voices within this debate.

The public framing of criminological questions and how a criminologist frames questions may be quite different. Indeed, as Thompson shows us, exploring why particular deviant activities have become the focus for concern at given moments in time may *be* the criminologists' concern, as much as the deviant activity itself. Where there is apparent social agreement over the formulation of criminological questions, it is part of the criminologists' job to explore and unravel the constituent parts of that agreement.

What is required, as a criminologist, is more 'upstream thinking'. The following parable comes in various forms (this one is recounted by Stan Cohen in *Visions of Social Control*) (1985). Social workers are equated with life-savers standing beside a fast-flowing river. Every so often a drowning person is swept alongside. The life-saver dives in to the rescue, retrieves the 'client' and resuscitates the drowning person. Just as they have finished another casualty appears alongside. So busy and involved are the life-savers in all of this rescue work that they rarely have time to walk upstream and see why it is that so many people are falling in the river. What is necessary, it is argued, is to refocus upstream, and what is needed generally among social workers (and, in our case, politicians, criminologists and workers in the justice system) is more 'upstream thinking'.

So what sort of solution does the trip upstream produce? There are a whole variety of possibilities according to how one interprets the information available. One may conclude that the people are jumping in despite notices which indicate the hazards of the water and that their problems can be regarded as their own fault; or that they were persuaded to enter the water or perhaps pushed into the water; or that all paths actually lead into the river and they have no option; or that they are the victims of genuine accidents.

Whatever one's own perspective on the cause of the near drownings or, as it is an analogy, on what causes crime and criminality, it is not enough as a criminologist to claim immunity from analysing these issues by simply saying that one only responds to a narrowly defined act of illegality (in this case, falling into the river). In-depth analysis is required – what we are calling 'upstream thinking' – to stand back and consider the sources of problems and to engage in some interpretation and theorizing, on the basis of evidence, about the sources of behaviour.

Throughout this chapter there has been mention of a variety of types of knowledge, as well as with formal and informal definitions of crime. The justice system is society's vehicle for deciding and implementing *formal* definitions and control of deviancy. Hence, it is to that system that we now turn in more detail.

3

Knowing about the Justice System

The criminal justice system is the collection of agencies by which society formally defines deviancy and controls deviants. The system encompasses policing, the courts and systems of punishment. In this chapter we provide information about different criminal justice agencies and highlight key tensions and dilemmas in each area.

Why does a criminologist need to know about the criminal justice system? In many respects this seems to be like asking why a physiologist needs to know about the human body. For the discipline of criminology, the criminal justice system is where it all happens – or at least most of it! The question can be more usefully rephrased as *what* does a criminologist need to know about the criminal justice system?

Although there is no particular virtue in knowing the exact number of police officers or the exact number of probation officers, it is important to get a 'feel' of the system. In doing so, we need to consider two main features of the system – namely, 'process' and 'outcome'.

Most people focus on 'outcome': For example, what are the sentences that offenders receive, how many offenders end up in prison, how many non-custodial sentences are awarded, how many offenders are acquitted. These are important issues, but they are only part of the story. What is equally important is to know about the 'process' – what happens in the course of going through the system. In chapter 2 we showed how the official rates of crime are produced by those actions actually taken by persons in the justice system that define, classify and record certain phenomena (see section on 'The official story of crime'). Now it is time to consider these various players in the criminal justice system and the processes, outcomes, activities and tensions they face in their daily work.

- First, we consider the justice system as society's means to control deviants, which will provide a framework for thinking about the criminal justice system.
- Second, we provide an outline of agencies within the criminal justice system.
- Finally, we consider some important issues that underpin the working of each area and, hence, of the criminal justice process.

The social control of deviants

Fundamentally, the criminal justice system has many of the characteristics shared by other organizations. The founding father of the sociology of organizations, Max Weber (1864–1920), analysed the most widely recognized and most commonly maligned form of organizational structure: bureaucracy (see box 3.1). Throughout his work Weber stressed that the bureaucratization of political and economic society was the most significant development in the modernization of western society.

As anyone who comes into even a brief contact with the criminal justice system would soon recognize, it is a vast industry of activity – lots of people coming into contact with the system without necessarily showing up in crime statistics. However, a vast range of activity is also true of, say, the National Health Service – allegedly the largest employer in Europe since the demise of the Red Army.

The strength of Weber's analysis is to show how these large organizations – and other organizations in the public and private sectors – have some considerable similarities. In many respects bureaucratic organizations are the same the world over.

We now want to take one step further and argue that the organizations set up to control deviants have certain similarities. Deviance can be considered as some form of undesirable difference, and criminals are only one kind of deviant – from a religious standpoint a deviant is someone who has sinned, from a medical standpoint a deviant is someone who is sick, and so on. In recent years there has been a considerable amount of discussion in western countries about

---

BOX 3.1   KEY FEATURES OF WEBER'S BUREAUCRATIC ORGANIZATION

1   A specialized division of tasks, undertaken by officials, each with his or her own duties.
2   A hierarchy of authority – 'a clearly established system of super- and sub-ordination in which there is a supervision of the lower offices by the higher ones' (Weber, 1968: 957) – and a clearly demarcated system of command and responsibilities.
3   A formal set of rules governing operations and activities which co-ordinates behaviour in a predictable, uniform and impersonal fashion.
4   A body of officials who are permanent, full-time workers, appointed by superiors, trained in a specialized task, paid a salary according to rank in the hierarchy, and to whom a career is open on the basis of ability and superiority.

Source: N. Abercrombie and A. Warde with R. Deem, S. Penna, K. Soothill, J. Urry, A. Sayer and S. Walby, *Contemporary British Society*, 3rd edn (Cambridge: Polity, 2000)

---

the social control of deviants. The family or immediate social group has a role in controlling deviance, usually referred to as the informal social control network, but most interest has centred around the development of more formal networks that exist within a community for assessing and controlling deviants.

The two major systems of social control in industrialized societies are the criminal justice and mental health systems. Psychiatrists, for example, have traditionally been operating as agents of social control in the mental health system but have a much more marginal role in the criminal justice system. In fact, some of the greatest dilemmas in the management of deviants have been raised at the interface of the two systems – issues of liberty and confinement, ethics and efficacy of the psychiatric treatment of offenders and so on. However, those concerns cannot be addressed here. We are more interested in pointing to the similarities in the procedures of the two systems.

Whatever the procedure, there is potentially a logical progression for the deviant from the time that behaviour first comes to the attention of formal social control agents to the time that the deviant is released from official control. Five analytically distinguishable stages in the process of control and management of deviants can be identified, although it is important to recognize that not all deviants need be involved in all stages (Soothill et al., 1981). The stages of the process are as follows:

- *Discovery* – what happens when certain behaviour is noticed.
- *Official screening* – when officials decide on the correct procedure to pursue and the nature of the deviant label to be imposed.
- *Disposal* – when officials describe what is actually to be done with the person.
- *Release* – when the question of a person's release from official control is decided.
- *After-care* – whether there are any formal arrangements to assist a person in settling down in the community.

Erikson pointed out that 'the community decision to bring deviant sanctions against an individual is not a simple act of censure. It is a sharp rite of transition, at once moving him [sic] out of his normal position in society and transferring him into a distinct role' (1964: 16). Erikson noted some of the ceremonies that accomplish this change of status, and the labelling involved is very much part of the criminal justice system, which we will now focus upon. The following discussion is adapted from Annex E, 'A day in the life of the criminal justice system' (Home Office, 2001). Criminologists do not need to remember the detail of what follows; the aim is to provide an overall impression of the workings of the system.

Outline of the justice system

The police

The scale of policing in any westernized nation is enormous. Nationally, police strength stands at around 124,600 officers. These officers operate from the 2,099 police stations in England and Wales. On average the police respond to around 25,500 '999' calls each day. Of these 15 per cent require an immediate response, while the remainder are graded as less urgent.

Every day, nearly 3,500 people are arrested on suspicion of committing notifiable offences, with a further 1,750 people being arrested for less serious matters, generally of a public order nature. An arrest does not necessarily result in official action. Indeed, it is estimated that no further action is taken against nearly 950 of those arrested each day. Around 2,400 are charged or summoned and 735 cautioned.

A contentious part of police work in recent years has been the stop/search procedure. Every day about 2,235 stop/searches are carried out, mainly by officers on uniformed patrol duty, on persons suspected of carrying drugs or stolen property. Around 290 (or 13%) result in an arrest. Meanwhile, around a quarter of the nearly 14,500 notifiable offences recorded by the police on any given day are cleared up.

The Crown Prosecution Service

Once the police have begun proceedings, the case is passed to the Crown Prosecution Service (CPS). Lawyers review the file and decide whether to proceed with, amend or drop the charges. Increasingly, this initial review is being carried out on police premises soon after the charge is made, so that the defendant may make a first court appearance within days of the charge.

Around 1,400 CPS lawyers operating from 96 offices in the 42 criminal justice areas are engaged each day in the work of reviewing files, preparing cases for prosecution and presenting cases in the magistrates' courts. Crown prosecutors are assisted by around 3,000 administrative staff. Although certain CPS lawyers have some rights of audience in a crown court, the bulk of higher court work is undertaken by barristers instructed by CPS staff. Each day, around 500 barristers are presenting the prosecution case in crown courts up and down the country.

So what of the caseload of the CPS? The huge majority (95 per cent) of criminal cases are dealt with in magistrates' courtrooms. Every working day, the CPS finalizes nearly 5,500 cases in the magistrates' courts. Of these, all charges are dropped in around 670 cases (or 12%). A further 350 are committed to the crown court, because the charges are so serious that they can only be dealt with there (nearly 150 cases daily) or because in triable-either-way cases the magistrates decline jurisdiction (about 140 cases daily) or because the defendant elects crown court trial (about 60 cases daily). Additionally, around 450 cases are dealt with in other ways – typically by being 'written off' when a defendant has failed to appear and has not reappeared or been rearrested within a given timescale. This leaves around 4,000 cases each day, which are dealt with entirely by magistrates' (including youth) courts.

Magistrates' courts

The great majority of magistrates' court cases – 3,930 – result in a conviction, the greatest proportion (nearly 90 per cent) following a guilty plea. Court business is conducted either by benches of lay magistrates (currently there are around 31,000), who generally sit in benches of three and are advised by legal advisers employed by the courts, or by professional district judges (of whom there are 106 full-time and 169 part-time). Where defendants are aged under 18, their cases are generally dealt with by the youth court.

There is much activity at magistrates' courts and youth courts, for each defendant appears an average of 2.2 times in relation to a particular case. On average, about 16,600 defendants appear in the magistrates' courts each day, and each day, 46 per cent of magistrates' court hearings result in an adjournment. Where an adjournment occurs and the defendant is remanded to appear at a future date, 85 per cent of defendants are remanded on bail and 15 per cent in custody.

Nearly 600 witnesses attend magistrates' courts each day to give evidence. Of these, around 340 are actually required to do so. Each one waits on average just over one hour before giving evidence.

Over 5,300 defendants are sentenced each working day in the magistrates' courts. Of this total:

- 3,960 are fined;
- 524 receive community penalties;
- 232 receive an immediate custodial sentence.

The remainder are dealt with in a number of other ways, but mainly through conditional discharges.

Crown court

The volume of activity in the crown court is much less than in the magistrates' courts. The 78 crown court centres in England and Wales deal with just 5 per cent of all criminal cases. However, these are typically the more serious and complex cases. Roughly 365 court-rooms are sitting daily up and down the country.

On average, around 350 defendants committed for trial make their first appearance in the crown court each working day. Of these, about 250 are committed on bail and 100 in custody. The eventual outcomes of their cases are as follows:

- 220 plead guilty;
- 45 are found guilty by a jury;
- 28 are acquitted by a jury;
- 7 are acquitted at the judge's direction at the end of the prosecution's case;
- 50 have their cases dropped before trial, written off or agree to a bind-over.

Approximately 4,400 jurors are called each day; of these, about 3,350 are requested to sit. On average, around 465 witnesses attend the crown court each day to give evidence in criminal trials; of this number, around 225 are actually required to give evidence. Just over half wait for two hours or more to give evidence.

Around 309 defendants are sentenced each working day in the crown court (either following conviction there or committal for sentence from magistrates' courts). Of this total:

- 61 per cent receive an immediate custodial sentence;
- 27 per cent receive community sentences;
- 4 per cent are fined.

The remainder receive discharges or other disposals.

Youth offending teams

Youth offending teams (YOTs) are a recent addition to the machinery of justice in England and Wales. Membership usually consists of probation officers, social workers, police officers, a health authority representative and someone nominated by the chief education officer for the area. There are now 154 YOTs, covering all of England and Wales. YOT members are engaged in a variety of work with young offenders, such as:

- assessing and managing the risk of re-offending;
- providing bail information and support services;
- preparing pre-sentence and other court reports;
- supervising community sentences and reparation orders;
- dealing with the rehabilitation of juveniles subject to police warnings;

- dealing with the parents of juvenile offenders under parenting orders;
- helping excluded children get back into school.

These are early days in the development of YOTs, but the scale of activity can be gauged:

- 840 offences each day resulting in some form of substantive outcome (e.g. sentence, final warning or reprimand);
- nearly 300 police reprimands and final warnings;
- nearly 300 young offenders sentenced;
- 42 of the following kinds of orders imposed each day: parenting orders; reparation orders; compensation orders, bind-overs and fines imposed on parents; and anti-social behaviour orders.

Victim Support and the witness service

Victim Support exists to provide comfort and assistance to victims of crime. It is staffed by a mix of paid employees and volunteers. The police automatically pass the details of victims of burglary, assault, robbery, theft (except theft from and of cars), arson, harassment or damage to a home to Victim Support. For certain other categories – sexual offences, domestic violence and homicide – referral is made only with the victim's consent. Victim Support staff may then contact the victim, either by telephone, in writing or in person.

On a typical day, the police will refer 3,000 victims to Victim Support. Victim Support attempts to contact all victims referred and is successful in 97 per cent of cases. However, not all who are contacted take up the offer of help. Victims are helped in a variety of ways: every day, on average, 441 victims receive a visit from a Victim Support volunteer, 67 receive an office appointment and 400 talk to a volunteer or member of staff on the telephone. Those who are not contacted in person will receive a letter providing information and offering further support.

Witnesses to crime – many of whom will also be victims – who are required to attend court to give evidence are also eligible for assistance both at court and prior to attending. The Witness Service (which comes under the umbrella of Victim Support) now exists at all crown court centres and the service is currently being extended to magistrates' courts. Currently 28 per cent of magistrates' courts (114) have a Witness Service. Every working day, approximately 345 witnesses are assisted in the crown court throughout England and Wales. Help may take the form of pre-court familiarization visits or advice and support on the day of trial.

Probation Service

The Probation Service carries out several key functions in the criminal justice system, including the preparation of reports for the courts to assist them in deciding on the most appropriate sentence, supervising offenders given community sentences and supervising offenders on release from prison. Nationally, there are 7,520 probation officers operating from 948 offices.

Courts may ask probation officers to prepare either a pre-sentence report or, when they have a particular sentence in mind, a specific sentence report. The former is usually prepared within fifteen working days; the latter will usually be available later on the day that they are requested. On a typical working day, the Probation Service prepares around 900 pre-sentence reports.

Each day, a total of 218,342 offenders are under some form of criminal supervision by the Probation Service, whether as a result of court orders or pre- or post-release supervision. Every day, around 171 offenders who have served custodial sentences of a year or more begin a period of supervision in the community upon release from prison. On average, each probation officer will be responsible for supervising sixteen released prisoners.

Daily, around 485 convicted offenders begin community services supervised by the Probation Service. The average caseload of each probation officer is around 37 offenders on supervision.

Prisons

There are 136 custodial institutions in England and Wales, housing a mix of convicted prisoners and remand prisoners awaiting trial or sentence upon conviction. Out of the total, 41 are young offender institutions, eight of which hold females. Three are solely for juvenile males (aged 15 to 17), while ten hold both juvenile males and young offenders. The Prison Service employs around 44,000 staff. The average number of prisoners per staff is 1.5.

Around 375 prisoners under sentence enter prison each day. Of these, 347 are male (267 adults and 80 young offenders) and 28 female (23 adults and 5 young offenders). In addition, the prisons receive on a daily basis around 336 remand prisoners who are awaiting trial or, having been convicted, are awaiting sentence. Of these, 309 are male and 27 female.

In 1999 the average daily population of prisons in England and Wales was around 64,770 (51,690 under sentence, 12,520 on remand and 560 non-criminal). Of the sentenced prisoners an average of 43,350 were adults and 8,340 young offenders.

Mandatory drug-testing has been operating in all custodial institutions since April 1996. In 1999–2000 14 per cent of random tests proved positive for at least one drug.

Mentally disordered offenders

Where an offender is suffering from a mental disorder that makes prison an inappropriate disposal, the court has the option of imposing a hospital order, with or without restrictions on discharge from hospital. Some offenders are initially sentenced to custody but are transferred from prison to hospital when either the nature and extent of their mental disorder becomes apparent after they have begun a prison sentence or where their disorder develops after sentence. Those receiving restriction orders will sometimes begin their sentences in one of England and Wales's three special hospitals (Broadmoor, Rampton or Ashworth); others will be assigned to psychiatric hospitals with secure units. On a typical day, four mentally disordered offenders are admitted from the courts to one or other of the above institutions on hospital orders. Additionally, about one offender a day is transferred after sentence from a Prison Service establishment to hospital.

The criminal justice process – key issues

By now it will be clear that there is a lot going on in the criminal justice system and many players – victims, offenders, witnesses and 'experts' (and many others not mentioned, such as journalists who report the main crimes or local court reporters whose reports fill the pages of local newspapers). However, there is little to suggest in what we have said so far that there are many underlying tensions that characterize the criminal justice process. These may be at the personal level – prosecuting and defence counsel may simply not like each other; there may be inter-professional rivalries – police and the Probation Service may have different ideas about supervision and surveillance;

or the tensions may reflect more fundamental 'philosophical' issues – in brief, what is it they are trying to do? It is to the latter that we now turn.

The following discussion is not exhaustive – there are many other issues to confront in considering criminal justice systems – but these are important ones that are difficult to resolve. What a criminologist needs to recognize is that such issues do not suddenly arrive unannounced; they often have a long historical pedigree. The British historian Philip Guedalla (1889–1944) once said: 'History repeats itself. Historians repeat each other' (Guedalla, 1920). What perhaps really happens is that some underlying tensions are never resolved. One historical period fails to clear up its baggage before it is replaced by the next historical period. We highlight such crucial, often historical, dilemmas at the very heart of the criminal justice system by focusing on:

- issues in contemporary policing;
- the courts;
- punishment.

Most attention is paid to policing, for it is an issue that lies at the heart of ideas about social organization and crime control.

Issues in contemporary policing

Undoubtedly policing is a difficult job. Indeed, the task can be life threatening and even routine policing can be very stressful. However, it is difficult for other reasons too. It is not entirely clear what the police are supposed to do and whom they are supposed to serve. The police seem to have many people looking over their shoulders. Peter Manning (1971) has commented that the audience for the police is diverse. In brief, the police must:

- convince the politicians that they have used their allocated resources efficiently;
- persuade the criminals that they are effective crime-fighters;
- assure the broader public that they are controlling crime.

To understand some of the dilemmas they face, we need to consider: the foundations and development of policing; the discretion exercised by the police; and the impact of the concept of 'law and order' on policing.

Development of policing   The development of the modern police force can be seen as a response to the crisis in urban administration that occurred in early Victorian Britain. Industrial capitalism created new sources of tension in the expanding towns and cities. There had to be a way of resolving this tension, for the police could not be seen as simply the agents of the rich and wealthy. What has emerged is that the British police have had to learn how to combine two distinct and complementary functions. First, they are the agents of a moral ideology that is represented in terms of their neutral and purely 'expressive' function of 'community welfare'. While this function can be derided as simply helping old ladies across the road, the public also expects the police to act in this 'welfare' way when they report their problems to the police. Second, however, they can also be seen as the agents of the dominant political and economic interests, and an explicitly 'repressive' function begins to emerge when they become involved in policing picket lines or breaking up demonstrations.

The early development of the police is related to the office of the constable: there was collective responsibility for his appointment and duties while he was in charge during the day. During the night there was something equivalent to a citizens' nightwatch. In contrast to the present police, the concerns of the nightwatch were more closely related to the general welfare of the citizenry, for example, looking out for fires, reporting the time and the weather and so on. By around the early 1800s, in most industrialized societies – and particularly in the larger cities – the constabulary had changed from being an essentially voluntary position to a quasi-professional one, that is, the constable was appointed and provided with an income.

One version of the history of social control is that there has been a transition from 'constabulary' to a 'police society'. This transition is typified by the proliferation of criminal laws, more and more enforcement officials, more use of criminal courts and prisons. It is argued that these changes were to the benefit of the powerful and wealthy, rather than for general welfare. There are varying views as to why the British police developed in the way it did. Certainly, controlling the effects of economic inequality was a major concern. Following the Industrial Revolution, the increasing economic specialization and the resulting 'class stratification' (that is, a division into various social and economic classes) can be seen as a primary cause for the development of the police. The role of the police in riots – riots usually being an attempt by the have-nots to challenge those with wealth and power – became crucial.

Hence, it has been argued that the police became an agency of those with wealth and power. The professional police gave the upper classes an extremely useful and powerful mechanism for maintaining the unequal distribution of wealth and power. More specifically, this position asserts that the law that is proclaimed to be for the general welfare is, in fact – by this kind of analysis – an instrument of class warfare. This approach is essentially the Marxist position, but there are other positions to argue.

Others see the police in the role of the referee, the neutral arbiter of disputes without fear of or favour to any one side. It is a nice idea and not entirely lacking substance. However, it is not so much the police we need to consider in this respect but the law itself. After all, a major part of policing is the enforcement of the law. From a Marxist position the law is seen as the instrument of the powerful to further oppress those without power. It is a bleak vision. However, an alternative position is to see the law as some sort of bulwark or defence against the powerful. Without the safeguard of the law, there could be no end to unfettered oppression. In other words, the law does delineate the boundaries of acceptable behaviour, and the task of the police is to marshal those boundaries. In so doing, the police are expected to be neutral arbiters. The police officer recognizes the dilemma. A tabloid newspaper will occasionally pick up the story of a chief constable stopped by one of his own police officers after a pleasant evening made even more pleasant by a glass or two (or was it three?) of good vintage wine. One can imagine the embarrassment of the police officer who stops his chief constable's car. Ultimately, reconciling the dilemma is a test of the use of discretion.

Exercising discretion   The police have an amazing amount of discretion. The important point is that the police officer is not, and never has been, simply a 'law enforcement officer'. In almost all circumstances they have discretion about whom they will arrest or investigate. 'Discretionary justice' occurs whenever decisions are made in criminal cases and these decisions are not legally or practically open to re-examination or review. If the intoxicated chief constable is allowed to make his way home and no one talks, then that decision is not open to review. Both parties would consider themselves unlucky if they happened to be followed by a tabloid journalist who was also at the dinner.

So what is the concern about the exercise of discretion? In the first place, discretion means that the police are certainly not enforcing all laws and punishing every violation. In the second place, police are enforcing some laws against some offenders some of the time. Discretion can be abused and there is particular concern to establish whether or not there is systematic bias against some groups in the community. Considering whether the police tend to favour some groups in society over others or whether they are neutral arbiters is a crucial issue.

Certainly, the experience of police behaviour differs quite dramatically between different groups in society. Do middle-class residential areas tend to experience only welfare aspects of police work, and are working-class districts the recipients of both repressive and expressive police attention? This potential difference in experience gives rise to a whole spectrum of statements about the police, ranging from 'all coppers are bastards', through 'there's some good coppers and some bad' to 'British police are the best in the world'.

Law and order   The terms 'law' and 'order' are often used together like 'eggs and bacon'. They sound as though they are interchangeable. But they are not.

One task of police public relations is to promote and emphasize the welfare, consensual role. In the media this role was probably first portrayed systematically in the famous TV series that started in the 1950s, *Dixon of Dock Green* (see chapter 2). So, on the one hand, the police have a welfare function, which – in theory and mostly in practice – is carried out impartially throughout society, irrespective of class, colour, age or creed.

But it is undoubtedly rather a different story with the other side of the job, which is to search and destroy classes and groups who are seen as 'dangerous', or in some way as a threat to the established political, moral and economic order. Indeed, alongside policing crime, what some see as the other task of the police has remained – maintaining public order. This raises dilemmas for the police when there are riots or even peaceful demonstrations (see box 3.2).

Consider what may have happened when there are complaints about police behaviour. When we read about – or see on our television screens – individual acts of police brutality, it sometimes may *really* be the case that a few authoritarian police officers have given vent to their particular prejudices and hang-ups. How could such individual actions be interpreted as structural or systemic problems?

Every police officer faces a dilemma, which is typified in 'street' situations: is their task to uphold the law or to maintain the peace? Both, everyone is likely to say. But what happens when these two sets

BOX 3.2   JULIET BRAVO

In the 1980s she was Britain's favourite TV cop. Last week she was detained during the May Day demos – until a policeman recognized her and let her go.

An unlikely spokesperson has emerged for the anti-globalization movement. Step forward Juliet Bravo, no-nonsense TV copper turned victim of overzealous policing at London's May Day demos last week. The actress, Anne Carteret, who played Inspector Kate Longton in the series for three years from 1983, was detained in Oxford Circus last Tuesday for five hours until, recognized by a policeman, she was freed. Her several thousand fellow demonstrators were forced to remain for a further three hours. 'We were protesting peacefully, which is every citizen's right, and always has been', says Carteret. 'Until, suddenly, this country became a police state.' . . . The civil rights group Liberty has condemned the police operation as 'unlawful' and will be announcing measures against the Met later this week.

Carteret had been invited to take part in a demo against the World Bank by her daughter, who campaigns for fair trade and who helped organize last Tuesday's events. While evidently no militant, the actress is a veteran of the Aldermaston CND marches in the 1960s. On this occasion, she was lobbying for the cancellation of Third World debt.

The actress likens May Day's demo to the Glastonbury Festival. 'There was a mixture of people, but they were all harmless. They were distributing leaflets, they were throwing fake American dollars in the air, they were playing music, singing, chanting. It was all peaceful.' The police clearly disagreed. 'Immediately they surrounded us and, for the rest of the afternoon, they would not let us out. They wouldn't even let little groups out; even women with children. Why? What did they think we were going to do? What crime were they preventing?' . . .

What particularly shocks her, having worked closely with police during her time on Juliet Bravo, was their behaviour. 'They were not interested in the fact that we were people.

> They stood like blocks of iron, not daring to express their opinion because they had their orders. I nearly burst into tears at the frustration of not being able to get through to them.' . . .
>
> She clearly still can't believe it. 'I think they see themselves as serving not the public but the government, and when they're told what to do, they don't think beyond that. I had hoped they did, but I have my doubts now.' . . .
>
> Eventually Carteret was able to persuade one PC to release her from Oxford Circus. 'He said, "I recognize you, you're Juliet Bravo, aren't you?"' . . . She is aware that selective favouritism towards celebrities (gossip columnist Nicky Haslam also escaped) is not a hallmark of good policing. So will Carteret attend future demos? 'I will', she insists. 'I will. People mustn't feel threatened if they want to speak or protest about something they care about. I had thought this was a civilized era of history.'
>
> *Source*: Adapted from *the Guardian*, 9 May 2001

of ideals conflict? This is what Skolnick (1966: 6) has called 'the tension between the operational consequences of ideas of order, efficiency and initiative, on the one hand, and legality, on the other'. This is the basic tension of police work that is rarely recognized but is crucial to understanding the policing of a particular society. In a totalitarian state, maintaining order is paramount, while in a society whose ultimate consideration is the protection of individual liberty within the framework of the law, upholding the law is paramount. In reality, most societies experience both kinds of policing.

The courts

The concern here is whether the court system does in reality match up to the ideals portrayed in the legal textbooks. Several American legal theorists have contrasted two models of criminal justice, which they have termed as:

- the due process model;
- the crime control model.

Packer (1968) likened 'due process' to an obstacle race: there are legal safeguards for the accused and a case will be thrown out unless, in legal terms, it measures up to the highest standards. 'Crime control' is more like an assembly line, with a steady stream of cases. The main priority is to try to control crime and so some legal niceties may be downplayed.

In the USA it is much clearer what is happening: after the preliminary hearing (when the accused is held for prosecution) the defendant may be offered a 'deal' by the prosecutor so that, if the defendant pleads guilty, he/she will be allowed to plead to a reduced charge. This, in American jargon, is the opportunity to 'cop out' to a 'knocked-down' charge. Where such informal methods are used to achieve a result, the roles of the various participants are co-operative rather than combative. The question that began to be raised in the 1970s was whether such interactions take place in this country also.

In Britain, the tension between the 'crime control' and 'due process' models in court procedures is a very real one. It would appear that in the most serious cases, such as murder, the accused enjoys all the possible legal safeguards. Some high-profile cases that get widely reported in newspapers seem to go on for weeks, and it is sometimes difficult to imagine what engages the court during all this time. 'Due process', then, would appear to be paramount, for certainly the prosecution does not want to lose their case on a legal challenge at appeal. In contrast, observation at some magistrates' courts would suggest that the crime control model seems to be more to the fore and that speed is of the essence. The combative theory of criminal law involving, in effect, a legal battle between prosecutor and defence seems much less in evidence, for around 90 per cent of the defendants plead guilty.

A critical issue is the use of plea bargaining. The term 'plea bargaining' refers to agreements between prosecution and defence in which concessions are offered to the accused in return for a guilty plea. A crucial study by Baldwin and McConville revealed that plea bargaining operates in crown courts in England and Wales. When the study was published as *Negotiated Justice* (1977), strong protests were voiced in the senior echelons of the legal profession, and the then chairman of the Bar said that publication of the book would be 'directly contrary to the public interest' (Baldwin, 1985). However, subsequent research has confirmed the importance of plea bargaining in the administration of English criminal justice.

A series of high-profile cases that were later adjudged to be miscarriages of justice seriously damaged the standing of British justice, highlighting concerns that the system was not working satisfactorily. The three cases that came to dramatize public concerns about policing most vividly were those of the Guildford Four, the Maguire Seven and the Birmingham Six. In all three cases, Irish suspects were convicted of causing explosions that killed multiple victims. The problems start when the media exert immense pressure on the police to get 'results' and then corners are cut. By the early 1990s public confidence in the police and the courts had eroded to such an extent that a Royal Commission on Criminal Justice – the first Royal Commission for fourteen years – was appointed in 1991 to inquire into the procedural issues involved and suggest remedies. Certainly the tensions between a court system where the paramount value is upholding the law through 'due process, and a court system which is seen as a crucial part of crime control were recognized. Nevertheless, the outcome was disappointing to many for, although the commission produced a large number of detailed recommendations, some of the real concerns were not faced. Lacey (1994: 41) pointed out:

> the really basic questions – questions about the social and economic conditions which foster crime; about the patterns of social division which mark out the social groups against whom criminal justice is enforced and, equally importantly, those against whom it is *not* enforced; about the long-term implications of a socially divisive 'law and order' politics, supported, in effect, by both major political parties; about the proper functions of the criminal justice system in a society such as ours; about the nature and future role of policing and police culture; about the values underlying the presumption of innocence – are simply not on the political agenda in this country.

Punishment

Penology (that is, the study of punishment in relation to crime) is a practically oriented form of social science that emerged in the early nineteenth century and, as Garland (1997) comments, developed alongside the prison and other institutions of modern criminal justice which were emerging around this time. The essential problem with penology is that it takes the existing institutions for granted and, while it has a critical dimension in identifying problems with the system, its overriding aim is to suggest rather piecemeal improvements and ways of enhancing the system's effectiveness. Hence, there is really no scope within this tradition to raise basic questions about

---

BOX 3.3   WHAT IS PUNISHMENT?

While the rules of societies, organizations and, say, families may differ, Walker argues that, underlying all these varieties of social institutions, there seems to be a shared conception of punishment, which has seven features:

1   It involves the infliction of something which is assumed to be unwelcome to the recipient.
2   The infliction is intentional and done for a reason.
3   Those who order it are regarded as having the right to do so.
4   The occasion for the infliction is an action or omission which infringes a law, rule or custom.
5   The person punished has played a voluntary part in the infringement, or at least the punishers believe or pretend to believe that he/she has done so.
6   The punisher's reason for punishing is such as to offer a justification for doing so.
7   It is the belief or intention of the person who orders something to be done, and not the belief or intention of the person to who it is done, that settles the question whether it is punishment.

Source: Adapted from N. Walker, *Why Punish? Theories of Punishment Reassessed* (Oxford: Oxford University Press, 1991), pp. 1–3

---

the ways in which society organizes and deploys its power to punish. Penology, then, usually fails to address the question 'why punish?'

'Why punish?' is a different question from 'What is punishment?' (see box 3.3). Social decisions about what constitutes punishment interact with justifications for punishment, but it is not exactly the same debate. The 'why' question has always been problematical – or at least since the beginning of the nineteenth century when these debates began to be aired – and we need to recognize that this is another important tension that underpins the criminal justice system.

The common notion that the punishment should fit the crime is essentially derived from what is known as the *retributive* rationale for punishment. The core idea in this rationale is that our system of justice was created to take the place of private vengeance. The retributive rationale is that the individual offender must be punished because he or she deserves it. In other words, retribution sees punishment as an end in itself. One of the problems in focusing exclusively on the crime rather than the criminal is that one would punish a person suffering from a mental disorder with the same severity as somebody who does not; similarly, one would punish a boy of 14 years for whom this is the first offence with the same severity as a 30-year-old man for whom this is his twentieth conviction. So, while simply punishing for the crime seems straightforward, there would soon be a public outcry if this approach were carried out without any consideration of who the offender was.

An alternative view is that punishment should be seen more as a means to an end, and the aim of punishment should be the prevention of crime in the future. In broad terms, the retributive rationale is probably more consistent with a view of the criminal as rational, and the preventive rationale, with certain exceptions, is more consistent with the view of the criminal as being less responsible for his or her behaviour. What has happened is that the view of criminals has changed many times over the course of history.

Theorists such as Quetelet (1796–1874) and Guerry (1802–1866) began to modify the classical position (hence their title as neoclassicists). Quetelet and Guerry recognized that some groups of people could not be held entirely responsible for their actions and therefore believed that they should not be punished. Into this category come the insane and the young who, they thought, should be treated differently because they were considered to be moral infants and did not possess the sense to refrain from wrongdoing.

When the positivists came to the fore in the second half of the nineteenth century, they proved to be the most powerful influence of all in terms of penological thinking: the positivist school influenced thinking to the extent that all criminal acts were believed to be merely symptoms of an underlying pathology. As we have already seen (chapter 1), Lombroso saw crime as something akin to a medical model – a disease model. Identifying crime as a disease means that a person is under the control of such disease until appropriate measures are taken.

This approach has been reflected over the past 100 years or so in the assumption that it is appropriate to try to do something to offenders to reduce their criminal activity. That 'something' can vary enormously. The 'something' may involve treating a psychological problem, such as a supposedly sociopathic or paranoid personality;

or addressing social problems, such as alcoholism and addiction; or resolving more pragmatic problems, like chronic unemployment, with vocational training in prisons, say, and job placement.

The tensions that surrounded sentencing in the nineteenth century remain as poignant in the twenty-first century: Is one sentencing the criminal or for the crime? Is one sentencing as retribution or to try to prevent more crime in the future? Some of the language about punishment may have changed. Nowadays the contrast is usually between consequentialism (i.e. forward-looking, what is going to happen in the future) and a 'just deserts' standpoint – that is, punishments based on non-consequentialism (i.e. reviewing the past, what has happened).

The tension resulting from competing expectations about the uses of punishment can produce public concern way beyond the criminal justice system. The killers of young James Bulger were given parole in 2001. The murder of an infant by children attracted particular disgust and outrage. Hence, many thought that when the offenders were released they had not served long enough for the dreadful crime they had committed (a non-consequentialist argument); the parole board, on the other hand, seemed to be looking much more to the future (a consequentialist argument), appearing to maintain that any further incapacitation could reduce their chances of settling down satisfactorily in the future.

Conclusion

Key agencies in the criminal justice system actively define, classify and record criminological phenomena in the course of their daily work. Together, they are society's formal system for defining and controlling deviants and deviancy. It is not surprising, then, that we find that these essential justice agencies reflect and make manifest society's tensions and confusions around every part of the justice process and every outcome of agencies' decisions.

These tensions are not new. Rather, they recur in new forms as societies change and they emphasize particular criminological problems and dilemmas. We have seen that discretion in decision-making is an integral part of the justice system, but this leaves it open to accusations of bias as well as wisdom. Where are we now in the ever-changing see-saw between justice and injustice? In the next chapter we will explore some of these issues further.

4

Whose Justice Is It?

Justice implies fairness; yet criminologists have questioned whether all members of society are treated equally by the justice system. Ethnicity, gender and age are all factors which, at some stage, have been explored with concerns about justice in mind. Rather than focusing on crime in isolation, such analysis places criminological explanations within the wider social and political framework.

Justice is a complex word. It is a measured recalibration after harm done, the exercise of authority, and a sense of fairness and balance. It implies the innate rightness of some outcomes or decisions over others; hence justice is a description of the decisions taken within the justice system. It is, in this last sense, about process and morality rather than just legality, although it is often meant in a legalistic sense. Yet legalistic justice is a system, a code of practices, of formal punishment and retribution. 'Balance' can be the recalibration after harm has been inflicted illegally, but it is more than retribution (the price exacted against harm done). Justice, in this sense, represents notions of fairness, equity and rights, not least those of the 'little people' against the powerful state.

Most people have heard of the signing of the Magna Carta, the great charter of English political and civil liberties, but few have realized its significance. When King John summoned the barons to meet him to sign the Magna Carta at Runnymede in 1215, it was to quell a revolt of the barons. This revolt against the Crown resulted in the first major attempt to obtain good laws and government for the whole country and for every class of people. The struggle which fills so many pages of English history continues to the present day and is essentially about trying to ensure justice when a subject comes into collision with the state.

The Magna Carta, with its 63 clauses, is the first definite statement in writing of the duties of the king and the rights and liberties of the subject. Most important, it defined limits to royal power. This did not stop the wars between John and his barons (indeed, civil war followed immediately after the signing of the charter). But it was the first formal acknowledgement of the public power struggles between winners and losers and of the place of laws and constitutional arrangements. Traditionally, it has been this public justice with which criminologists have been concerned: justice as a political event, the public exercise of power and the confirmation of social order.

Two opposing viewpoints

Public justice is at the heart of political society. Within democratic societies there is an ideal of ruling through consensus and agreement, and in Britain this is symbolized by legislation passed to address social issues. Enfranchisement – that is, the right of individuals to vote – is one achievement of democracy; but so, too, is the invention of electoral systems whereby power can change hands with limited violence and without loss of life. This is essentially the *liberal–democratic theory of the state*, expounded in and derived from the work of philosophers such as Hobbes, Rousseau and Smith. This theory maintains that a 'plurality of interests' has been achieved in modern capitalist societies by the separation of the legal and political systems from the direct influence of economic interest (Hall and Scraton, 1981). It is this 'separation of powers' which supposedly prevents the state from assuming an oppressive function. Hence, the pluralist view sees the state's policies and laws as capable of pursuing justice equally and fairly, without serving particular class interests. Where justice is not delivered equally and fairly, this is seen as a problem that needs to be rectified.

There are other theories that are much less sanguine about the state's role. 'Instrumentalist' theories, which develop from the Marxist tradition, make the economic relationship their central point of reference, pointing to the state as an instrument of the capitalist classes and to law as the property of the capitalist class.

Hence, on the one hand, the 'rule of law' is the means whereby the least powerful sections of society can seek a redress for their grievances. Yet, on the other hand, the 'rule of law' can be understood as a contradictory element that has been used both to oppress and to protect the poor and other disadvantaged groups. Certainly, the relationship of the law to the state is an extremely complex one. During periods of comparative social stability, the law is able to maintain its 'separateness' from state influence. But once a major threat to social order is perceived, then the state is able to use the legal form to protect its interests. So, for example, during the 1984/5 miners' strike there were concerns about the ways in which the police were using their legal powers to try to control the situation. Was what they were doing always 'legal' (Scraton, 1987)? In such a situation the law must reconcile its immediate interest in maintaining order with the long-term interest of maximizing its legitimacy. The role of the police in such troubles becomes critical. In theoretical terms, one asks: are the police the neutral upholders of the law (liberal–democratic theory of the state), or do they exist in order to enforce a 'law and order' which maintains the present structural inequalities ('instrumentalist' theories)?

Unequal access to justice

Democratic rituals replace conflict in the exchange of public power. Violence within the political arena is now usually associated with civil war, international war or terrorism. Force is always the brute exercise of power by one person or group over another, and distinguishing between legitimate and illegitimate force within democratic states remains a complex matter. Furthermore, in the absence of violence disempowerment becomes hidden and covert. It needs to be recognized that disenfranchisement lies as much in unequal access to justice as it does in not being able to vote. Justice, in its crudest sense, can be whatever the state legitimizes – even if this is not always accepted as moral by all the people living under that system (see box 4.1).

It can sometimes be easier to see how particular groups are not protected by law through examples from history; indeed, to see how members of particular groups are endangered or systematically disempowered by legal systems and laws. The famous rabbi Hugo Gryn, and Robert Maxwell, the infamous newspaper tycoon and

BOX 4.1   JUSTICE FOR ALL?

Justice for all is a fine-sounding concept, but for the past 100 years it might be better summed up by the phrase 'justice for some, sometimes'. For much of the past century, rich men have done well out of the legal process, and poor women fared worst.

In its outward trappings, the law has not changed much in 100 years. Judges and barristers still wear the same kind of horsehair wigs, robes and gowns sported by their predecessors a century ago.

A century ago, divorce was so expensive, and such a complex procedure, that only the very rich could afford it. The poor were more likely to commit bigamy than get divorced. Few would have foreseen the arrival of what is, in effect, divorce on demand.

At the beginning of the twentieth century, using the law and the courts to enforce rights was largely the preserve of the rich. Solicitors looked after the landed classes. Legal aid, introduced in 1950, opened the courts to all in one of the biggest social changes of the century. Now, with widespread cutbacks in state financial support to assist legal actions, the large middle-income group no longer qualifies.

Before legal aid for criminal cases, defendants who could not afford to pay resorted to the 'dock brief'. Any barrister robed and sitting in court could be hired for £2.10s. With the coming of legal aid, defendants facing serious charges were able to hire the top criminal barristers, paid for by the state.

Public confidence in the police and the criminal justice system took a severe knock in the 1980s and early 1990s, when a series of miscarriages of justice came to light. Most notable of these were the quashing of convictions of the Guildford Four in 1989 and the Birmingham Six in 1991. The legacy of these cases has been to introduce stronger safeguards for defendants and an improved system for referring cases to appeal.

Source: Adapted from 'Law' by Clare Dyer, *Guardian*, 19 June 1999

publisher, both eventually settled in London but grew up in sub-Carpathian Ruthenia. This remote area of Europe has at different times been a part of Hungary, Czechoslovakia, Germany, the USSR and, more recently, the Republic of Ukraine. Overnight, in 1938, it was switched from the control of Czechoslovakia to that of Hungary. Hungary introduced the 'Jew Laws', and it was these laws which gave a legal rationale to the later deportations of Jewish people from the area. This led Hugo Gryn to experience labour camps and forced marches. Maxwell saw action in the British army, ending the war in Berlin where he made contacts that led to his post-war career as a publisher. Both lost family, friends and neighbours through the Nazi labour and extermination camps. The actions taken against the Jews of sub-Carpathian Ruthenia were legal, in that the laws of the lands concerned made legal provision for them (see Gryn, 2001; Bower, 1991). Hence we see that laws may not protect certain groups but, indeed, actually authorize violence against them.

Unequal access to legal protection and to justice is not always so obvious or directed, and criminology can explore these indirect and sometimes hidden inequalities. Are there some groups whose members are more stringently policed, prosecuted and punished by society than others? Are such individuals less protected by the law when they are victims of crime? Criminologists have questioned how an individual's relationship with justice and the justice system has been affected by their membership of particular groups or categories. To explore these themes, we focus particularly on the issue of ethnicity, and then on gender and age.

Ethnicity

Members of ethnic minorities tend to have a different relationship with the criminal justice system according to whether they are regarded as potential offenders or potential agents of control, such as the police, the magistracy or the judiciary. Among the former they are seriously over-represented; among the latter they tend to be under-represented.

Some people come into contact with the justice system through being prosecuted, which can lead to conviction and penalties, such as fines and prison sentences. But many more are cautioned, stopped in the street and searched, and many arrests are made which do not proceed to prosecution. Hence numerous people interact uncomfortably with aspects of the justice system and do not appear in 'criminal'

Table 4.1 Representation of ethnic groups in the criminal justice system (%)

	White	Black	Asian	Other
Population (10+ over)	94.5	1.8	2.7	1.1
Stops and searches	85.2	8.2	4.4	0.9
Arrests	87.0	7.3	4.0	0.8
Cautions	87.2	5.7	4.1	1.0
Prison receptions	86.0	8.5	2.5	2.9
Prison population	81.2	12.3	3.0	3.4

The rows may not add up to 100% as there were also 'not knowns'.
Source: Based on *Statistics on Race and the Criminal Justice System* (London: Home Office, 2000), Table A, p. vi

statistics. Rather than expecting different groups in society to be represented equally in *numbers*, the rates of representation of different ethnic groups need to be judged against their representation in the population as a whole.

Table 4.1 highlights the disproportionate representation of blacks and Asians at various points in the criminal justice system. The difference between the number of blacks in the general population and in the prison population is particularly marked. There are different ways of interpreting these figures. It could be that the black and Asian populations do indeed commit more crime, or it could be that they are more readily apprehended. These possibilities are not mutually exclusive and both could be happening.

Table 4.1 shows some quite striking differences. What we are concerned with here is how much disparity is the result of unequal treatment by the criminal justice system. In fact, there are various possibilities in explaining these differences that can be summarized as (1) direct discrimination; (2) uneven law enforcement; (3) legally relevant criteria; (4) subcultural behaviours; and (5) differences in offending rates (Smith, 2001). These explanations need to be examined more fully.

1 *Direct discrimination* This would seem to be the most obvious and visible source of discrimination, but it is not always so easy to recognize. If the police search only nightclubs used by the black population, then this is direct discrimination (Smith, 2001).

However, this type of discrimination comes to light only if it is discovered that the police do, indeed, search only such nightclubs.

2   *Uneven law enforcement*   Police car patrols are much more visible in some areas than others. It is rare to see a police car meandering through the streets of leafy suburb areas. This is because they do not expect trouble there. Indeed, the residents of leafy suburbs tend to complain that they do not see enough of a police presence to deter potential burglars. The opposite is the case in some inner-city areas where many ethnic minorities reside. Police cars are present, ready for trouble. Their expectations are not unrewarded, but there is also a greater likelihood of mistakes being made. The 'stop and search' laws have been a particular focus of growing suspicion and developing hatred between police and policed in recent times (see Fitzgerald and Sibbitt, 1997).

3   *Legally relevant criteria*   What appear to be neutral laws and practices can cause disparity. In order to cope with the vast number of cases coming before the courts, there is a subtle encouragement for persons to plead guilty (Baldwin and McConville, 1977); one of the 'rewards' is a sentence reduction for a guilty plea. Hence, if members of an ethnic group more often plead not guilty, then the sentence – for those who are subsequently found guilty – is likely to be longer. There is some evidence that this may be happening.

4   *Subcultural behaviours*   Differences in behaviour between groups can be many and various. Some activity can make certain groups much more visible to the police. So, for example, if a subcultural practice is to meet one's mates informally on street corners, then members of this kind of group are at much greater risk from circulating patrol cars than those following a subcultural practice of meeting one's mates in the nearest kitchen. Outdoor activity in public space makes one much more vulnerable to both arrest and victimization than indoor activity in private space.

5   *Differences in offending rates*   While there is perhaps a general reluctance to suggest that some groups do have higher offending rates than others, this remains a real possibility. In the classic Chicago work of Shaw and McKay (1942), ethnic groups were shown to have high offending rates while they were stuck in the ghetto, but the rates changed when they moved into more desirable residential areas. It seems reasonable to suggest that the 'have-nots' in a society do have higher crime rates for certain types of crime than the 'haves'. The 'have-nots' are certainly more likely

to be involved in shoplifting than in white-collar crimes (such as fraud and price-fixing), whereas the 'haves' are more likely to be involved with the latter.

The figures in table 4.1, however, still do not complete the story of how many (and how often) members of ethnic groups come into contact with the justice system. People are arrested and prosecuted, but not all are successfully prosecuted or, indeed, go to court. Decisions by the Crown Prosecution Service to proceed with cases against young defendants show variations relating to ethnicity. Evidential grounds were the main basis for the termination of cases before court proceedings began (Asian defendants 74%, black defendants 63% and white defendants 60%). This suggests that some groups are more likely to be prosecuted when the evidence is much more slender.

Barclay and Mhlanga (2000) have shown that white defendants were more likely to be convicted (78%), than black (69%) or Asian defendants (68%), who were more likely to be acquitted or have their cases terminated early. Barclay and Mhlanga note that the pattern was similar even allowing for variations in rates according to type of offence. This is puzzling until one remembers that black and Asian defendants are more likely to plead not guilty and thus contest the charge. Unless one does contest the charge, there is no chance of being acquitted. By pleading not guilty more often, black and Asian defendants are both more likely to be acquitted *and* more likely to receive longer sentences if convicted.

While being apprehended by the police heralds one type of experience of the justice system, another type of experience can be gained through working within the system, in paid or voluntary roles. Here there is a different picture for members of ethnic minorities (see table 4.2). Home Office statistics on race and the criminal justice system (2000a) show 'low representation of ethnic minorities in all grades as employees in the police service, prison service and in senior posts in all criminal justice agencies' (p. 61). The exception is the Probation Service where black people, but not Asians, are quite highly represented. This presents at least two possibilities. First, the Probation Service is one of the services whose practitioners, as well as leaders, are perhaps more seriously committed to an equal opportunities policy than some others. Second, black people may be more willing to serve in an organization that is less strongly identified with control and traditionally more closely identified with the help and support of vulnerable groups.

Table 4.2   Known ethnicity of practitioners in the criminal justice
system (%)

	White	Black	Asian	Other
Population (10+ over)	94.5	1.8	2.7	1.1
Police (all ranks)	97.8	0.8	0.7	0.7
Prison officer	97.4	1.5	0.7	0.4
Prison governor/equivalent	99.2	0.4	0.2	0.2
Probation (all grades)	90.7	7.0	1.3	1.0
Victim Support (all)	91.0	4.4	2.9	1.7

The rows may not add up to 100% as there were also 'not knowns'.
Source: Based on *Statistics on Race and the Criminal Justice System* (London:
Home Office, 2000a), pp. 62–5

Within the courts, the picture is no better. Ninety-five per cent of
lay magistrates are white; there are no black or Asian High Court
judges or Lord Justices; one of the 568 circuit judges is black and
three are Asian; and sixteen of the 1,329 recorders are black and eleven
are Asian. The higher ranks in the hierarchy are much less likely to
have representatives of ethnic minority groups. Among all types of
solicitors the rates of representation for black practitioners never
goes above 3 per cent, or above 4 per cent for Asian practitioners (see
Home Office, 2000a: 62–4).

Being directly involved in the criminal justice system – whether as
offenders or as social control agents – affects only certain members
of minority ethnic groups. Everyone's perspective on justice depends
in part on how safe one feels within society, and being subject to
crime undermines an individual's security and their trust in the system
to provide protection. The 1996 British Crime Survey showed that
members of ethnic minorities were more likely to be victimized than
white people. About 15 per cent of the crimes committed against
them were assessed as racially motivated. In addition, the British Crime
Survey estimated that some 200,000 black or Asian people 'experienced some form of racially motivated victimisation or harassment
in 1995' (Percy, 1998: 1); and, perhaps not surprisingly, the survey
found that members of ethnic minorities perceive themselves to be

at greater risk of crime than whites, worry more about falling victim
of a crime and [feel] less safe on the streets or within their own homes

at night. To a large extent this is a reflection of their higher risks of victimisation and harassment. (Percy, 1998: 1)

There is a tense interaction between ethnicity and the criminal justice system, and this should be a cause for concern. We cannot feel confident that ethnic minorities receive justice or participate fully in dispensing justice. In some respects, the Stephen Lawrence case brought matters to a head. Stephen Lawrence was an 18-year-old student who was stabbed to death in south London. It became evident that the murder was motivated by racism, but the police activity was brought into question. The Macpherson Report which investigated the case was hailed as a watershed. In particular, the Macpherson Report drew wider attention to the problem of institutional racism within the police force – that is, the collective failure of the police to provide an appropriate service to people because of their colour or ethnic origin. More recently, a report into race discrimination in the Crown Prosecution Service has found that a significant number of ethnic minority staff are being discriminated against (Denman, 2001). According to the author of the report, ' "institutional racism" has been and continues to be at work in the CPS' (p. 108).

Gender

In terms of women's representation, crime is not an equal opportunities area. Men traditionally commit more crime than women and commit more serious crime. The true extent of women's victimization remains a contentious issue, given the ambiguity surrounding society's views of domestic and sexual violence. The justice system remains primarily an employer of men.

With an analysis based on Home Office figures, Heidensohn (2000) has summarized women's known participation in crime as offenders. She concluded 'that there is still a considerable gender gap in criminality', whatever measures are used:

In 1997 only 17 per cent of the known offenders dealt with by the British criminal justice system were female. In general women are likely to have shorter careers in crime, are less liable to be convicted for repeat offences and their most common indictable offences (accounting for 59 per cent of female offenders in 1997) are theft and handling stolen goods. (Heidensohn, 2000: 35)

Table 4.3 Female sentenced population and receptions in 1999 by crime category (%)

	Sentenced population (on 30.6.99)	Reception (1999)
Offence type		
Drug offences	36	14
Violence against person	18	12
Theft and handling	17	39
Burglary	7	4
Robbery	7	3
Fraud and forgery	5	8
Sexual offences	1	–
Motoring	1	5
Other	8	15

Source: Based on *Statistics on Women and the Criminal Justice System* (London: Home Office, 2000b), pp. 27–8

Table 4.3 shows the difference between the crime profile of the sentenced female prison population, many of whom will be serving longer terms, and the number of *receptions* in a year, which will reflect the numerous short sentences received by women (see discussion in chapter 2).

While women are more likely to be received into prison under sentence for theft and handling, fraud and forgery and drug offences, men are more likely to be sentenced for violence against the person, sexual offences, burglary, robbery and motoring offences (Home Office, 2000b: 28). There is a different profile of offending for men and women. Women offenders rarely outnumber male offenders, other than for minor offences such as prostitution.

There are also other differences between the sexes. Whereas women are far less likely to be arrested than men, women are more likely to be cautioned because they are 'far more likely than men to admit their offences and more likely to be arrested for less serious offences (e.g. shoplifting)' (Home Office, 2000b: 9).

All this begins to raise familiar questions concerning the equality of men and women in the criminal justice system. Mary Eaton (1986) in her thoughtful book *Justice for Women?* was one of the first to raise these questions in relation to the court arena. Following her research at the anonymized Hillbury Court, she concluded that:

within its own terms Hillbury Court treats men and women equally, i.e. they receive similar sentences when they appear in similar circumstances. However, men and women rarely appear in similar circumstances – the differences in their recorded criminal involvements are as marked as the differences between the sexes in other areas of life. *Formal equality within the strictly defined area of the court does not affect the substantial inequality of women and men who appear before the court.* (Eaton, 1986: 97, emphasis added)

Eaton's argument is an important one. She maintains that the inequalities that women experience elsewhere in society are endorsed by what she terms 'the process of cultural reproduction operating within the court' (1986: 97). She examines the familial ideology that underlies summary justice and maintains that this reveals that women are not equal to men in court, since the court is operating from a perspective which defines women as different and subordinate. Eaton argues that the family circumstances and disposable income were rarely similar for men and women and that this affected the sentences. Her message is that, while the evidence of similar treatment for the few men and women who appear before the court in similar circumstances may satisfy the *court's* criteria of justice, this has little to do with the way in which the subordinate role of women is reproduced by the very processes of the court. Gender divisions are endorsed by the judicial process (see box 4.2), the crucial point being that women lack justice in society in general.

The growth of the women's movement in the 1970s led to increased awareness of women as victims in ways that are different from the experiences of men. Home Office figures draw on the British Crime Survey for material on violent crime. Changes to the 1996 survey (especially the switch to a computerized self-completion questionnaire) show how feminist writings, in particular (but also developments in victimology) have influenced survey design. There is increased awareness of the need for sensitivity when attempting to gain access to information about domestic and sexual crimes in interviews:

The self-completion questionnaire increased respondents' willingness to report incidents by maximising anonymity and confidentiality. It also encouraged reporting of incidents victims did not define as 'crime'. (Home Office, 2000b: 37)

In reality, for those women who experience physical violence or sexual violence, the offender is likely to be someone that they know or,

BOX 4.2   JUSTICE AND EQUALITY

Should justice be blindfolded?

For feminists campaigning during the nineteenth century and in the early years of the twentieth century the law was a clearly recognized area around which to organize their demands. There were legal obstacles, as well as social attitudes and customs, limiting the aims and aspirations of women. On matters relating to family duties and responsibilities, on access to education and jobs, on control over income and property, on political recognition, feminists fought to achieve the status of adults, with the same rights as adult men. However, even during this period when legislative reform was clearly necessary, there were debates on the meaning of 'justice' and 'equality' for women. While some argued for equal treatment, others wanted positive discrimination which recognized, and sought to redress, the existing inequalities.

The question is still with us. The Equal Pay Act and the Sex Discrimination Act both define 'equality' for women as parity of treatment with men. Both acts employ a concept of justice based on uniform treatment rather than positive discrimination. This concept of 'justice' is also found within the criminal justice system. Individual or class differences are not officially recognized by the law and while many argue that the courts respond favourably to those with wealth and resources, there is no provision for explicitly redressing the balance for those who appear before the court already disadvantaged in relation to the rest of society. On the contrary, there is pride in the knowledge that the figure of justice – the embodiment of the British legal system – standing above the Central Criminal Court in London, is blindfold, and so cannot distinguish between the individuals who come before her.

However, to accept that 'justice' and 'inequality' are to be achieved by parity of treatment is to collude in the acceptance of the inequalities that co-exist with such 'equal treatment'. To assume that justice for women means treating women like men is to ignore the very different existences which distinguish the lives of women from the lives of men of similar social status.

Source: Adapted from M. Eaton, *Justice for Women? Family, Court and Social Control* (Milton Keynes: Open University Press, 1986), pp. 10–11

Table 4.4 Percentage of respondents subject to domestic violence, 1999/2000

	Women (aged 16–59)	Men (aged 16–19)
At some time in life:		
assaulted by partner	23%	15%
threatened	26%	17%

Source: Based on *Statistics on Women and the Criminal Justice System* (London: Home Office, 2000b), p. 38

indeed, may be living with at the time they fill in the questionnaire. This 'private' image of crime is at odds with the traditional view that 'real crime' is something that occurs only between strangers.

This latter view 'is likely to inhibit the revelation or recognition of much physical or sexual violence committed against women' (Zedner, 1997: 583). Hence, table 4.4 is likely to be a barometer of such crime rather than an absolute picture.

Women were estimated to comprise 33 per cent of all homicide victims in 1998/9. While this demonstrates that men are in greater danger from homicide than women, it needs to be recognized that 33 per cent of these women were killed by current or ex-partners, whereas this was the case for only 8 per cent of men (Home Office, 2000b: 38).

Certainly, the experiences of many women as offenders and victims are different from men, but what of gender comparisons in terms of those working in the criminal justice system? Walklate reviews the figures (see table 4.5) and concludes that although numbers of women are increasing (in, for example, the police), justice remains predominantly men's work (2001: 10).

As with ethnicity, Walklate argues that such limited representation of women in the justice system impacts on women offenders and victims as well as workers. Not only does it shape what is expected of women workers but notions of gender impact 'upon the qualities expected of their male colleagues' (2000: 11). It matters because:

entering such a male-dominated world implicitly, and often explicitly, structures the experience of that world for women who enter it as either victims or offenders. Stereotypical expectations of appropriate

Table 4.5   Women working in the criminal justice system

Policewomen (1998)	16% of force
Barristers (1998)	26%
Queen's Counsels (1998)	7%
Solicitors (1998)	34%
Prison officers (1999)	14%
Magistrates (1999)	49%
Circuit judges (1999)	14%

Source: Based on S. Walklate, Gender, Crime and Criminal Justice (Cullompton, Devon: Willan, 2001), p. 10

> feminine behaviour can pervade the judgements made about particular women who enter it. Stereotypical expectations of appropriate masculine behaviour can also pervade the decisions made by those working within the system. (Walklate, 2001: 11)

This analysis moves beyond looking at justice from the standpoint of the few women engaged with the justice system to conceptualizing ways in which the social construction of gender (rather than the biological categorization of sex) constrains both men and women.

Age

Age is of crucial importance when we consider how people interact with the justice system. Crime is strongly associated in the public mind with the activities of young people, and many criminological theories focus almost entirely on juvenile delinquency. Certainly, official statistics show that a disproportionate number of offenders are found among the young. According to a recent Home Office report, in 1999 there were 145,700 known male offenders between the ages of 10 and 17 in England and Wales, and 35,900 female offenders within the same age group. The peak age of offending is currently 18 for males and 15 for females (East and Campbell, 2001).

The same Home Office report draws on figures from the Youth Lifestyles Survey (YLS) to illustrate the extent of self-reported offending among young people aged between 12 and 30 living in England and Wales (see table 4.6).

Table 4.6 Proportion of young people who admitted committing any offence *in the last 12 months*, by age group (%)

Age in years	Males	Females
12–13	15	12
14–15	33	18
16–17	26	16
18–21	35	15
22–25	28	8
26–30	19	7

Source: C. Flood-Page, S. Campbell, V. Harrington and J. Miller, 'Youth crime: findings from the 1998/99 youth lifestyles survey', Home Office Research Study 209, Home Office, London, 2000

Almost a fifth (19%) of 12–13-year-olds admitted at least one offence *in the last 12 months*, although young women were less likely to have offended than young men. The figures outlined in table 4.6 are often referred to as *the age-crime curve*. In other words, if we were to plot the same numbers on a graph we would see a curve. This curve illustrates that involvement in crime tends to escalate during the teenage years, but declines during the twenties. (Of course the age-crime curve is much less marked for women than it is for men, simply because female offending rates are never that high in the first place).

Criminologists often refer to the age-crime curve as a justification for focusing their attention on young offenders. However, self-report data with older people indicates that the age-crime curve is not in fact constant across all offence categories. Presenting data from the Cambridge study in delinquent development, Farrington (1989) notes that while offences such as vehicle theft may decline dramatically with age, the offence of 'theft from work' actually increases with age. Recent research shows that 33 per cent of males and 9 per cent of females born in 1953 had been convicted of at least one 'standard list' offence before the age of 46 (Prime et al., 2001).

In trying to understand the disproportionate representation of young people as offenders in official statistics, we need to accept that a great deal of crime is indeed committed by young people. However, it is also worth pointing out that the activities of young people are much more easily policed than those of adults. Pearson notes that 'young people are under more rigorous systems of control and surveillance, principally through the institutions of the family and the school, with the result that their actions are more publicly accessible and observable than those of adults' (1994: 1193). In addition, young people have less access to private places and so their crimes are more visible, being likely to be committed in public spaces, particularly out on the streets. This also affects detection rates. Police patrol public spaces but need permission to gain access to private places.

Although it is understandable that much more attention and resources are given to controlling the public activities of youth – for these raise anxieties, particularly among older people – it may be at a price. Focusing extensively on youth offending may result in a comparative neglect of the crimes of the powerful. We take this issue up in chapter 7 when we consider the importance of white-collar crime. For now however, it is worth noting that a focus on the activities of the young is certainly a preoccupation among policy-makers. The majority of new measures introduced in the Crime and Disorder Act 1998 were directed at young offenders, leading some to suggest that it may have been more appropriate to call the new legislation a Children and Young Persons' Act (Piper, 1999).

In recent years, there has been a particular concern about the perceived threat of children who are 'out of control', although Pearson's *Hooligan: A History of Respectable Fears* (1983) indicates that such concerns are not new. It seems there were football hooligans well over a hundred years ago. Yet, paradoxically, while society does have a tendency to demonize its youngest members, there is also heightened concern about protecting children from becoming victims.

In their study of young people in Edinburgh, Anderson et al. (1994) found that criminal victimization is a common feature of many young people's lives. Yet they noted that experience of victimization tends to remain hidden from adults, including both parents and police. Similarly, Aye Maung (1995) found that relatively high levels of victimization were reported by 12–15-year-olds in the 1992 British Crime Survey. She concluded that there was some evidence to suggest that victimization rates were higher for this age group than for adults.

A Home Office report (Kilsby, 2001) provides some further useful material:

- In a ten-year period (from 1989 to 1999/2000), the number of notifiable offences for child abduction increased from 140 to 577.

- Over a one-year period (from 1998/9 to 1999/2000), the number of notifiable offences for cruelty to, or neglect of, children increased from 2,300 to 2,631.

However, it needs to be recognized that changes in the above figures may well reflect changes in reporting and recording levels and increased awareness of the offence itself, rather than an actual change in the underlying levels of crime. For example, constant scandals concerning physical and sexual abuse of children in residential care were exposed throughout the 1990s and have undoubtedly raised public awareness in this area.

So, for example, in the wake of the North Wales care home scandal and the subsequent government inquiry (Waterhouse, 2000), there was relentless media attention and initial public disbelief over the horrendous sex crimes that had been exposed. One of the key questions asked was how such abuse could continue undetected for so long. Mike Taylor, head of children's services for the NSPCC, was quoted in an article in the *Independent on Sunday* as explaining the situation in the following way:

> The public perception was that they were children who were dangerous or delinquent and that was why they were in care. They were also not to be believed because the people they were making allegations against were very important members of staff. (Dobson, 2000: 16)

The North Wales experience indicates how ready we are to apply the label of 'villain' to those who are already vulnerable. It supports the main message of this chapter that those without power can find it much more difficult to obtain justice.

Discussion

Underpinning this chapter has been the concern as to whether different groups get fair and equal treatment from the criminal justice system. Even more important, not only do they but also should they? Does equal treatment mean identical treatment? A fine of £100 for a white-collar offender may mean very little in pecuniary terms but will be more than some impoverished defendants possess in the world. Is this equal treatment? Such analysis takes us far away from Lombroso's assumption that criminals are a separate group of people; rather, it places understanding of crime and criminality firmly in a social context.

People who come into contact with the justice system are not a random collection of individuals. Some groups have more contact with the justice system than others. This is true not only of those apprehended by the law but also of those who administer justice. The former tend to be over-represented in terms of young males and members of ethnic minorities; the latter tend to be dominated by older white males. In contrast, women have an anomalous position in the justice system. In terms of numbers, they are under-represented as offenders, yet there is still concern that they do not get fair treatment. In the administration of justice women tend to have the lower status jobs, although some claim this is changing.

For some theorists (e.g. Hagan, 1994) social class is *the* crucial explanatory variable in understanding crime and social order. All this may well be true, and it serves to highlight the point that factors other than age, gender and ethnicity are also important when considering what happens in the work of the criminal justice system.

However, what has been missing from this chapter has been an exploration of interdependent and interactive factors. *Individual* people are not male *or* young *or* white but a combination of these factors. In other words, they may be a young Afro-Caribbean female from a relatively low socio-economic background; or they may be a young Asian male from a middle-class background who, as a victim of crime, is looking for legal redress.

Individuals do not necessarily experience crime and safety as relating to discrete, individual events of victimization or offending, but rather as interrelated elements in an environment in which they perceive themselves to have greater or less autonomy. Lack of power to protect oneself against crime is, indeed, a part of poverty and disadvantage and shapes a person's respect for justice and the capacity or concern of the justice system to protect individuals who are recognizably like themselves. A 'sense of justice', then, is a shorthand expression for one's interaction with the wider society. In short, a sense of justice or a sense of grievance arises out of one's whole relationship with society rather than out of edited highlights.

Is the role of criminology to explain crime or to promote justice? Howard Becker famously challenged his academic colleagues to consider 'Whose side are we on?' (1967). The central thrust of Becker's challenge was the assertion that it is impossible for social scientists to do research that is 'uncontaminated by personal and political sympathies', and that, regardless of which theoretical perspective the sociologist adopts, they must write *either* from the standpoint of subordinates *or* from that of their superiors. One cannot do equal justice to both.

Of course, Becker's tendency to define offenders as 'the subordinates' is not an approach which all would agree with. It could be argued that the victim in each 'criminal event' should have first call on the attention and sympathies of the wider world. Notions of justice are always linked to morality – concepts of right and wrong – and hence to the need to take a stand. In this way a 'justice' approach undermines the idea that one can take a dispassionate view as 'onlooker', and indeed makes this seem undesirable. A 'justice' viewpoint raises doubts about whether crime can be understood independent of its social context, and questions whether or not criminality alone is the most effective route for understanding and explaining anti-social behaviour.

It was the social context of crime that haunted Henry McKay, one of the members of the early Chicago School, who questioned whether race and nationality had any effect on delinquent behaviour. His researches, with Clifford Shaw, originally answered the question firmly in the negative, repeatedly showing that the delinquency rates for each nationality were high only while the group resided in a slum or run-down area. As assimilation took place and the nationalities (Poles, Italians, Germans, Irish) dispersed to outlying areas of Chicago, their delinquency rates approximated to those of other groups. Thus, in their analysis, crime and delinquency are caused by the *social* conditions, not by racial and ethnic origins. It is linked to sites and situations, to the ecological and social situations confronted by the people who reside there (Shaw and McKay, 1942).

McKay's generalization broke down, however, when assimilation was not the natural course for black Americans. Stuck in the ghetto, black Americans had high crime rates that remained high over generations. This fact not only threatened the generalization but also implicated American society. Some groups, particularly black Americans, were not able to share the 'American dream' of upward social mobility. For McKay, the importance of the social context for crime was compelling. Is such social analysis still a legitimate part of criminology? Can crime be explained without exploring its context? Further, in Becker's framework (see box 1.2), a criminologist cannot comment on social inequity without taking sides, without commitment or without becoming involved.

Thus the question remains as to whether criminologists should seek to contribute directly to society's capacity for justice. If so, should this be through developing theoretical explanations of crime or through generating knowledge that relates more directly to society's perceived criminological problems? As we have already seen in chapter 1, there has long been a tension between criminology and policy-making, between research relating to the administration of justice and the process of theorizing (and we return to this issue in chapter 6). To those more concerned with *action* about crime, criminologists' theorizing can appear to take us further away from understanding criminological phenomena, such as crime, criminals and harm. However, we contend that theorizing is a very necessary step toward establishing credible explanations of crime and criminality. In the next chapter we look at the development of theory in criminology, and explore how it helps in the pursuit of a greater understanding of crime.

5

Explaining Crime and Criminality

Crime theories attempt to *explain* crime and criminality. Here we outline some key theories and questions that illustrate important moments in the development of criminological ideas. Rather than exhaustively describing all major crime theories, this chapter aims simply to introduce readers to the relevance of theorizing by adopting a questioning approach.

Numerous explanations of crime and deviance exist in contemporary society. Why do people commit crime, and what motivates them to do so? Such questions create controversy and debate among academics, politicians, the media and the general public, and competing explanations of crime are promoted.

Theorizing is something that most of us engage in every day. Most of us have our own ideas about how, and why, crime occurs. For example, when young children commit offences, attention and blame is frequently projected on to the immediate family. When young men become involved in late-night brawls, we almost expect that a large consumption of alcohol will have played its part. Such ideas and views may seem fairly commonsensical, but it is ideas like these that enable us to develop theories of crime.

A theory is an idea, a view or an assumption that allows us to make some sense of the world around us. Theories range from simple, straightforward assertions to highly complex and refined formulations, and it is always worth remembering that just because a theory is complex does not necessarily mean it is good. At the same time, theories that are too simple can have a limited explanatory value. We know, for instance, that some young men in late-night brawls may not have consumed any alcohol at all. Furthermore, alcohol alone is rarely the sole cause of aggression. Given that human beings are complex creatures, explaining the causes of criminality is often a difficult task. In relation to criminology, theories are attempts to make sense of why and how particular crimes occur at certain times and in certain places. They aim to explain rather than confuse!

Because there is no universal consensus over which are the best and worst explanations of crime and criminality, the numerous textbooks devoted to criminological theory can be overwhelming. Yet a brief glance through any textbook reveals that many theories are trying to explain completely different things. Some focus on individual-level causes of crime, such as low self-control. Others devote their attention to structural factors within the wider society, such as poverty and unemployment. Certain theories focus on particular types of crime, such as street crime, but pay no attention to crimes of the powerful. Other approaches are concerned with particular groups of offenders and focus on issues of race, gender, class and age. Clearly such theories are not in competition because they offer different levels of explanation.

What is clear is that a variety of different questions occupy the attention of criminologists. Sometimes these questions are based on quite different assumptions about human nature, crime and criminal behaviour. Furthermore, even if theorists are concerned with the same question, they may offer quite unrelated responses to it. Often it is easy to become bogged down in detail when we are trying to get to grips with specific theoretical explanations. On such occasions it can be useful to try and stand outside the detail and take a look at the big picture. What is the theory trying to explain? What question might this theory be a response to, and what are the assumptions underlying that question? In this chapter we suggest a number of approaches to questioning criminological theory, as ways of unravelling the explanations of crime that they offer us. First, we follow the traditional way of ordering criminological theory, by establishing a short history of ideas. We then approach 'interrogating theory' in two, alternative ways:

- by exploring key theories with specific, key questions;
- by making sense of theory with broader, categorizing questions which locate theories in time, place and school of thought.

The quantity of theory alone, before thinking about its diversity, can make the discipline seem fragmented to new students. So, later, we explore whether or not it is possible to produce a general theory of crime and then discuss issues relating to theoretical integration. Lastly, we establish which current theoretical approaches are influential in criminological thinking.

A history of ideas

Theories come and theories go, but some seem more able to withstand the test of time than others. In order to understand some of the popular explanations currently on the theoretical agenda, it is important to get a sense of what has gone before.

As we saw in chapter 1, many explanations of crime and criminal behaviour are underpinned by one of two particular views of human nature – classical theory or positivism. According to the classical position, individuals engage in a process of rational decision-making when deciding whether to commit crime. This belief is based on two basic assumptions:

- Human beings have free will.
- Human beings are guided by hedonism – the maximization of pleasure and the minimization of pain.

The task for criminal justice, then, is to ensure that the prospect of punishment is more painful than the rewards of criminal behaviour. In contrast to the classical school, positivists are primarily concerned with the search for scientific, observable facts about the causes of crime. Early work in this area focused on the causes of crime within individual biology, rather than on individual free will. Positivists explain crime by reference to factors that are outside of the decision-making ability of the individual. These two views run through the timeline illustrated in box 5.1, which summarizes the history of criminological theory. From 1970 onwards, we refer to the 'fragmentation of theory', in recognition of the fact that there have been a variety of influential approaches, rather than one dominant theory, since this time.

BOX 5.1   A CRIMINOLOGICAL TIMELINE

Some key dates		Some criminological landmarks
	1760	**DEVELOPMENT OF THE CLASSICAL SCHOOL**
		1764 Cesare Beccaria *Dei delitti e delle pene* ('On crimes and punishments')
	1780	1789 Jeremy Bentham *Introduction to the Principles of Morals and Legislation*
1801 First British census	1800	
	1810	
1821–3 Irish famine	1820	
	1830	
1840 Penny post started	1840	
1859 Publication of Darwin's *Origin of Species*	1850	1857 Dr Benedict Morel on degeneracy theory
	1860	
	1870	**DEVELOPMENT OF THE POSITIVIST SCHOOL**
		1875 Cesare Lombroso *L'Uomo delinquente* ('The criminal man')
	1880	
	1890	1892 Foundation of the Department of Sociology at the University of Chicago
1906 Labour Party formed	1900	

Year	Events / Theorists	Theory
1910		
	1914–18 World War I	
1920		
	1925 Ernest Burgess 'The growth of the city'	[CHICAGO SCHOOL]
1930		
	1938 Robert Merton 'Social structure and anomie'	[STRAIN THEORY]
1940	1939–45 World War II	
	1942 Clifford Shaw and Henry McKay *Juvenile Delinquency and Urban areas*	[ECOLOGICAL THEORY]
1950		
	1955 Albert Cohen *Delinquent Boys*	[SUBCULTURAL THEORY]
1960	***A CHALLENGE TO POSITIVISM***	
	1963 Howard Becker *Outsiders*	[LABELLING THEORY]
	1969 Travis Hirschi *Causes of Delinquency*	[CONTROL THEORY]
1970	***FRAGMENTATION OF THEORY***	
	1977 Richard Quinney *Class, State and Crime*	[MARXIST THEORY]
	1977 Carol Smart *Women, Crime and Criminology*	[FEMINIST THEORY]
1980	1984–5 Miners' strike	
	1986 Jock Young 'The failure of criminology: the need for a radical realism'	[NEW LEFT REALISM]
	1986 Alfred Blumstein et al. *Criminal Careers and 'Career Criminals'*	[CRIMINAL CAREERS]
	1989 Poll tax introduced	
	1989 John Braithwaite *Crime, Shame and Reintegration*	[REINTEGRATIVE SHAMING]
1990	1990 Michael Gottfredson and Travis Hirschi *A General Theory of Crime*	[SELF-CONTROL THEORY]
	1993 Robert Sampson and John Laub *Crime in the Making*	[LIFE-COURSE PERSPECTIVE]
2000		

Interrogating theory

Key theories and key questions

Rather than plodding through each set of theories represented in the timeline, in the following discussion key theoretical ideas are selected to illustrate how they can be understood as responses to different, specific questions. The questions we explore are:

1 What is the difference between criminals and 'non-criminals'?
2 What is the significance of the social environment in determining levels of crime and criminality?
3 Why don't we all engage in criminal behaviour?
4 How, and why, do certain activities get labelled as crimes, and certain individuals get labelled as deviant?
5 Is the criminal justice system prejudiced against women and ethnic minorities?
6 How can we distinguish between different levels of offending and different types of offender?

Approaching theory in this way highlights how ideas about crime and criminality are based on different types of explanation. Ideas can emerge as answers to different questions, but the questions themselves may be indicative of changing societal concerns over time.

1 What is the difference between criminals and 'non-criminals'?
This question assumes that criminals are significantly different from the rest of the population. It immediately establishes an 'us and them' relationship with those who engage in criminal behaviour. What distinguishes us from them? Early attempts to answer this question focused on biological and psychological factors within the individual, and therefore the explanations that followed generally adopted an individual-blaming approach. In other words, they located the causes of criminal behaviour within the individual.

Lombroso's ideas about crime were very much influenced by Darwin's work on evolution. According to Lombroso, criminals were evolutionary throwbacks who could be identified by certain physical attributes. This led to the idea of the 'born criminal' (see box 5.2).

Lombroso's image of the 'born criminal' paints an amusing picture. However, the idea of being able to identify criminals by their physical

BOX 5.2   LOMBROSO'S CRIMINAL MAN

Lombroso has recounted the moment of his key discovery about the criminal. . . . On a gloomy morning in the winter of 1870, he had been trying in vain to discover anatomical differences between criminals and the insane. He examined the skull of the famous brigand Vilella and suddenly he had a flash of insight. . . . In the brigand's skull he saw the traces of a past which should have been shed from modern Italy:

This was not merely an idea, but a revelation. At the sight of that skull, I seemed to see all of a sudden, lighted up as a vast plain under a flaming sky, the problem of the nature of the criminal – an atavistic being who reproduces in his person the ferocious instincts of primitive humanity and the inferior animals. Thus were explained anatomically the enormous jaws, high cheek bones, prominent supercilious arches, solitary lines in the palm, extreme size of the orbits, handle-shaped ears found in criminals, savages and apes, insensibility to pain, extremely acute sight, tattooing, excessive idleness, love of orgies, and the irresponsible craving of evil for its own sake, the desire not only to extinguish life in the victim, but to mutilate the corpse, tear its flesh, and drink its blood.

Source: Adapted from D. Pick, *Faces of Degeneration: A European Disorder, c.1848–c.1918* (Cambridge: Cambridge University Press, 1989); illustration from Cesare Lombroso's *L'Uomo delinquente*

appearance has rather sinister implications. As we mentioned in chapter 1, judges were ordering Lombrosian analyses of defendants' physiques as late as the 1930s!

Although Lombroso's theory is certainly dated, it is important to recognize that it was one of the earliest attempts to answer a question that has remained influential in modern criminology. The question is still being asked, but the answers are generally becoming more sophisticated. Certainly, new developments in the area of genetics and DNA testing indicate that the search for the differences between 'us' and 'them' is likely to continue into the foreseeable future.

2 What is the significance of the social environment in determining levels of crime and criminality?   In contrast, this question is based on the assumption that factors external to the individual, such as the social environment, may be influential in understanding crime and criminal behaviour. We would expect answers to this question to move beyond Lombroso's purely individual-level theories.

Some of the earliest answers to this question are attributed to the Chicago School (see chapter 1). In the early twentieth century, during a climate of rapid industrialization and mass immigration to the cities, researchers became increasingly preoccupied with the way in which

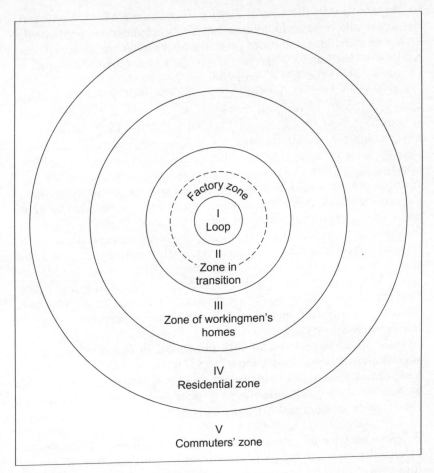

Figure 5.1 The zonal hypothesis
Source: E. W. Burgess, 'The growth of the city'. In R. E. Park, E. W. Burgess and R. D. McKenzie (eds), *The City* (Chicago: University of Chicago Press, 1925)

the layout of the social environment could affect crime. Researchers in Chicago focused on patterns of immigration and divided the city into different types of residential zone (see figure 5.1). One particular zone just outside the central business district was identified as the site of most social problems. This was described as the zone of transition.

The zone of transition was one of the least desirable places to live in the city, but it contained some of the cheapest housing and was close to the factories in the central district. Immigrants who were new to the city would be most likely to move into the zone of transition, with a view to moving out to more desirable zones when they could afford to do so. This focus on the social environment, which developed at Chicago during the 1920s, still continues.

Crime prevention initiatives in, for example, the UK are particularly concerned with identifying 'problem areas' and deprived housing estates. A report by the Social Exclusion Unit in 1998 outlined the government's national strategy for neighbourhood renewal, which aims to narrow the gap between England's most deprived neighbour-hoods and the rest of the country (Social Exclusion Unit, 1998).

Other attempts to determine the significance of the social environment on levels of crime and deviance have focused on societal goals and cultural aspirations. Robert Merton's 'strain theory' (1938) outlined the tension (or strain) that exists between cultural aspirations, such as financial success, and the structural opportunities that allow people to achieve such success. According to Merton, deviant behaviour is a symptom of the gap between cultural aspirations and access to acceptable means of achieving these goals. Hence, those who have few opportunities or means of achieving success are more likely to resort to illegal methods.

These ideas were subsequently influential in the development of subcultural theory. Albert Cohen (1955) noted that lower class youth have the same goals as mainstream society but often lack the means to achieve these goals. Membership of a delinquent subculture can therefore be an alternative means of achieving status.

3 Why don't we all engage in criminal behaviour? This question echoes the classical view of human nature that assumes we are all inherently self-interested, and it is the starting point for Hirschi's version of social control theory (1969). Rather than considering why people commit crime, the primary concern is in fact to understand why people do not. In rejecting the view that some special motivation is required for delinquency, such as membership of a deviant sub-culture, Hirschi offered quite a radical challenge to positivism. His approach suggested that many previous explanations of crime and criminality had been answering the wrong question.

Hirschi saw the delinquent as a person who was relatively free of the intimate attachments, aspirations and moral beliefs that bind most people to a life within the law. A person is free to commit delinquent acts because their ties to the conventional order have somehow been broken. In considering why individuals conform, Hirschi pointed to the influence of the social bond. One of the central elements of the social bond is attachment, which emphasizes sensitivity to the opinion of others. When parent/child attachments are strong, Hirschi argued, then it is less likely that the child will be delinquent.

4 How, and why, do certain activities get labelled as crimes, and certain individuals get labelled as deviant? Rather than taking crime and criminal behaviour as given, and assuming that certain acts are inherently criminal, this question has an entirely different focus from those already discussed. It is based on the assumption that crime is the result of a labelling process. This takes our attention away from why individuals do or do not commit crime and directs us towards societal reactions to certain types of behaviour. Certainly, the development of labelling theory in the 1960s took criminology in a very different direction from where it had been before (see 'A paradigm shift' in chapter 1), challenging many of the assumptions that underpinned previous criminological research. In particular, it emphasized the power of criminal justice agents, such as the police, in labelling certain types of behaviour and certain types of individual. There was also a concern with the stigmatizing effects of being labelled.

Other theories have focused more specifically on issues of power, arguing that the criminal justice system is used by the most powerful in society as a legitimate site in which to criminalize other social groups, such as the working class. This perspective is associated with critical criminology and Marxist theory. Commentators in this area have argued, for example, that police surveillance is generally focused on working-class communities, which means that crimes of the powerful, such as white-collar crime, are far less likely to be detected (e.g. Box, 1983).

While this approach has a long tradition – the Dutch criminologist Willem Bonger (1876–1940) is often seen as an early analyst – it is interesting to note that Karl Marx (1818–83) did not specifically address the issue of crime. Rather, his particular brand of social theory has been further developed and built upon, particularly during the 1970s, by criminologists such as Chambliss (1975) and Quinney (1977) – hence the category 'Marxist theory'.

5 Is the criminal justice system prejudiced against women and ethnic minorities? Developments in criminology during the 1970s placed questions of power quite firmly on the theoretical agenda. In many ways, critical theories and Marxist perspectives paved the way for more specific and focused theoretical formulations, such as feminism, to follow. Thus, a question about whether the criminal justice system is prejudiced against certain social groups can broadly be understood as an extension to the previous question on labelling.

(a) *Gender* Feminists in the 1970s pointed out that women had been completely neglected in the majority of theories of crime and criminal behaviour (Smart, 1977), a situation much changed in the last two decades (see Gelsthorpe and Morris, 1990). One of the key debates that has emerged concerns the treatment of women in the criminal justice system, and whether or not they are treated any differently from men (see chapter 4).

Feminist criminology has challenged the assumption that women often benefit from the chivalry of a male-dominated criminal justice system. According to this view, female offenders are more likely to be treated leniently by the police and the courts because they are women. However, commentators such as Pat Carlen (1985) suggest that because women's low share of recorded crime is so well known, those women who are actually found guilty of offences are often regarded as doubly deviant and treated as such. Criminal women are not only regarded as deviant because of the crimes that they have committed, but also because they have gone against traditional feminine stereotypes.

(b) *Race* How far there is racial discrimination within the criminal justice system is a contentious issue (as we saw in chapter 4), and notably one that has become particularly prominent in the UK during recent years. The murder of the British teenager Stephen Lawrence in 1993 provoked widespread debate over the existence of institutional racism within the police force (see chapter 4). On a related note, criminologists are increasingly preoccupied with the particular category of crime labelled 'racist violence', in recognition of the fact that racist motivations are a key factor in many violent offences.

6 How can we distinguish between different levels of offending and different types of offender? This question moves away from structural-level issues and turns our attention back to the individual offender. However, rather than focusing on the biological differences between 'us' and 'them' in traditional Lombroso fashion, the concern here is on the different pathways that individuals may take during

---

BOX 5.3   CRIMINAL CAREERS

According to the criminal career position, it is important to examine the sequence of crimes committed by individual offenders over time. This approach, as developed by Alfred Blumstein and colleagues (1986), seeks to identify different aspects of a criminal career.

Characteristics of a criminal career include:

- participation in crime;
- frequency of crimes committed;
- seriousness of offences committed;
- career length.

---

their career in crime. At one level we can respond to this question by documenting the differences between individuals according to the crimes that they have committed. In other words, we can identify sex offenders, murderers, drug dealers, joyriders and so on. However, there is an increasing concern among theorists in this area to move beyond the differences between crimes committed and actually try to identify different career patterns in crime.

According to Blumstein et al. (1986), frequency, seriousness and length of career can all vary considerably across offenders (see box 5.3). For example, at one extreme are those who commit only one offence throughout their lives. Yet at the other extreme are what the authors describe as 'career criminals' – those who 'commit serious offences with high frequency over extended periods of time' (1986: 1). Both extreme career types are considered to be of policy interest. Offenders who commit only one or two offences can be used to identify any external factors that may have caused them to put an early end to their career. Meanwhile, career criminals are of interest for formulating policies that identify such offenders early in their careers and attempt to prevent further criminality.

In Britain the most influential exponent of the 'criminal careers' approach is David Farrington. His prescriptions for some major intervention efforts are firmly grounded on empirical research results. The Cambridge study in delinquent development is a prospective longitudinal survey of the development of offending and antisocial behaviour in 411 boys, most of whom were born in 1953 and who, at the time, were all living in a working-class area of South London. They were first contacted in 1961–2 and continue to be followed up to the present day. Results of the study have been described in four books (West, 1969, 1982; West and Farrington, 1973, 1977) and in over 100 articles (e.g. Farrington, 1992, 1995). However, there are problems with the study. While 40 per cent of the boys in the study were convicted of criminal offences by the age of 40, the numbers are still comparatively modest on which to make wide generalizations. Furthermore, few boys in the study were from ethnic minorities, and the study tells nothing of the patterns of offending among females. Nevertheless, the study started when longitudinal surveys of this kind were very uncommon and the rigour of the work remains impressive.

Making sense of theory

Key questions have taken us a long way in interrogating some theories. But theories frequently appear under different categories and class-ifications, which often need to be understood in order to grasp the specifics of a theory. The idea of categorizing theories is to highlight some of their similarities and differences and illustrate how certain positions relate to one another. As Nisbet (1966) notes, theories can be discussed in relation to certain schools of thought (classifying periods of time), particular ideas and concepts (such as anomie) or the theorists themselves (such as Karl Marx). It is important to be aware that theories rarely develop in a social vacuum. The majority of us respond to current social concerns and trends in one way or another, and the criminological theorist is no exception. Hence most theories need to be understood in relation to the social context in which they developed.

So there are three basic questions worth considering when trying to get to grips with specific theoretical explanations.

1 What is the theory trying to explain, and therefore what aspects of the crime-criminal problem does it ignore?
2 How might we categorize this theory in relation to:

   • schools of thought/periods of time;
   • key concepts and ideas;
   • main theorists?

3   When and where was the theory written? What was the potential
    influence of the social context at that time?

In the following discussion we work through these questions using
two distinct theoretical approaches as examples. The first approach,
Merton's strain theory, can be regarded as a conservative theory, that
is, right-of-centre in political terms. By contrast, the second approach,
New Left Realism, is strongly associated with the political left.

**1 *What is the theory trying to explain, and therefore what aspects of
the crime-criminal problem does it ignore?***

(a)   Strain theory, as associated with the work of sociologist Robert
K. Merton (1938), locates the roots of crime and deviance firmly within
the structure of society. According to strain theory, there is a tension
that exists between cultural aspirations, such as financial success, and
the structural opportunities, such as education and employment, that
enable people to actually achieve such success. Structural inequalities
place many individuals, particularly the lower classes, in the position
of desiring what for them are unattainable goals. Merton suggests
that those who have few opportunities for achieving cultural goals
are more likely to resort to illegal methods and deviant behaviour.
    Strain theory is an explanation of deviant behaviour among the
disadvantaged and rejects the notion that the causes of crime lie
within the individual. However, strain theory does not address crimes
of the powerful – those who have legitimate means for achieving
success but still resort to deviant behaviour. Neither does strain theory
consider the importance of gender issues.

(b)   New Left Realism developed in Britain in the 1980s and is
generally associated with the writings of Jock Young (1986, 1992).
The theory emphasizes the importance of understanding the *reality*
of crime, its origins, nature and impact – hence the focus on 'Realism'.
The term 'New Left' is a reference to the political persuasion of
theorists emphasizing this approach. Realists argue that crime is a
real problem for everyone; it affects all classes, although victims most
commonly belong to the working class.
    This theory aims to provide a four-fold explanation of crime that
focuses on the victim, the offender, the reaction of the formal agencies
of the state and the reaction of the public. The emphasis on the importance of victims' experiences has been regarded as particularly useful,

given that so many other theories focus exclusively on offenders. However, although New Left Realism also asserted the importance of addressing issues of class, race, age and gender, it has been criticized for privileging class-based explanations (Walklate, 1998).

2 How might we categorize this theory in relation to schools of thought/periods of time, key concepts and ideas, and main theorists?

(a) Merton's strain theory is a *positivist* approach that locates the causes of deviance within the social structure rather than within the individual. It is also broadly regarded as a conservative theory, because it is based on the assumption that there is *consensus* in society over what constitutes culturally desirable goals.

One of the key concepts underlying this theory is the notion of *anomie*. In Merton's terms, anomie is defined as the disjuncture between societal goals and the acceptable means for achieving these goals. Deviance is regarded as a product of anomie.

While strain theory is widely regarded as emanating from the work of Robert Merton in the 1930s, it has recently been revisited and built upon by Robert Agnew (1992). Agnew's 'general strain theory' indicates that many of the ideas about society in the 1930s are still relevant today.

(b) Following criticisms that many Marxist and critical theories were too simplistic, New Left Realism emerged as a new form of critical criminology. However, it is still classified in the same way as its predecessors – as a *conflict* theory, which assumes that society is based on conflict rather than consensus.

One of the key concepts underlying New Left Realism is *relative deprivation*. This refers to understanding the conditions whereby people may not only be objectively deprived, but may also perceive themselves to be deprived in comparison to others. Realists regard experience of relative deprivation as an important cause of crime.

In addition to, and often alongside, Jock Young, Roger Matthews has been very influential in developing New Left Realist ideas in Britain (see Matthews and Young, 1992).

3 When and where was the theory written? What was the potential influence of the social context at that time?

(a) Writing in America in the 1930s, Merton was witness to the effects of the Great Depression, whereby large numbers of people were deprived of the opportunity to attain what they had been taught to desire. The so-called American Dream, with its emphasis on material affluence, financial prosperity and owning fast cars, was exactly what many aspired to. An inherent part of the dream was the idea that everyone had the opportunity to move from rags to riches; there were equal opportunities for all. Merton's theory convincingly dispelled this belief. In contemporary society, where the gap between rich and poor grows increasingly wider, it is arguable that strain theory has never been more relevant.

(b)   As Walklate (1998) points out, the social and political context in Britain during the late 1970s and early 1980s contributed significantly to the development of New Left Realist ideas. In 1979 the Conservative party was elected to office on a strong law-and-order ticket, under the leadership of Margaret Thatcher. Civil disturbances in various inner-city areas in 1981, combined with Thatcher's re-election in 1983, sharpened general debate on the crime problem. Disenchanted with the ability to reform society under the exceedingly right-wing, conservative direction of the government, academics on the political left began to search for alternative ways of talking about crime. Against this wider social context, New Left Realism emerged – a new theoretical approach with an overtly political perspective.

Interestingly, the examples used are normally classified as completely distinct and different approaches, yet working through the three questions reveals that they are in fact based on quite similar assumptions. In particular, Merton's concept of anomie sounds strikingly like Young's concept of relative deprivation. Commenting on strain theory in 1971, at least a decade before the introduction of New Left Realism, Steven Box actually argued that Merton conceptualized anomie as a condition of relative deprivation (Box, 1971: 105–6).

We have discovered that two distinct approaches written in two different countries in two different time periods – one regarded as a conservative theory, the other associated with the political left – are in fact based on surprisingly similar key concepts. Hence, it is arguable that this question-and-answer approach to understanding theory moves us beyond a standard textbook interpretation of theories of crime and deviance.

In addition, taking account of the wider social and political context in which an approach is developed brings theory to life, helping us to appreciate that theorizing is about individuals responding to

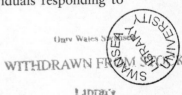

the society in which they live. In many ways crime theories are commentaries about the society of the time. So to make sense of theory requires more than an understanding of a set of abstract ideas; it means locating the theorist in a particular time and place.

Is it possible to produce a general theory of crime?

Given that there are so many different theories trying to explain so many different things, is it possible to produce a general theory of crime that can explain everything, answering all of the 'how', 'why', 'when' and 'where' questions that we have about crime and criminality?

One of the most contentious general theories put forward in recent years is Gottfredson and Hirschi's (1990) self-control theory. They argue that low self-control is the individual-level attribute that causes crime at all ages. Low self-control is equated with criminality and is regarded as a time-stable individual trait that tends to be set by about the age of eight, as a result of early socialization and child-rearing experiences.

While this theory has provoked considerable attention in the criminological literature, it has also been criticized on the grounds that it cannot be applied to all types of crime, especially white-collar crime and organizational offending. Certain types of organized crime may require detailed planning and forethought, and it does not logically follow that such offences result from impulsive and short-sighted behaviour that is characteristic of low self-control. One of the strengths of Gottfredson and Hirschi's theory is its simplicity. However, it is arguable that in simplifying, the authors have distorted the reality of the crime problem.

It is noteworthy that the second author of the general theory of self-control also put forward a highly influential social control theory at the end of the 1960s. Interestingly, Hirschi's (1969) formulation of social control theory (outlined above) had a somewhat different focus from his later work with Michael Gottfredson. The first position conceptualized control in relation to the strength of social networks within wider social institutions, such as the family and the school. Hirschi's later approach regards self-control as an attribute located within the individual, one that tends to be time-stable regardless of attachments to the wider society (C. Taylor, 2001).

Thus, not only do different crime theorists put forward different types of theoretical explanation, but the same theorist may put forward different types of explanation, as their understanding of crime and criminality changes over time. While Hirschi is certainly not the only crime theorist to have altered his theoretical position over the years, using the example of his two versions of control theory also highlights the issue of recurring themes in criminology. Are recent developments in crime theory telling us anything new, or are they simply trying to provide better answers to the same questions? Is it the case that we know all the important questions about crime and criminality, and we are in the business of trying to provide more sophisticated responses? Or are there other questions out there that have yet to be articulated, questions that may take criminology in quite different directions from where it has been before?

Returning to the discussion of general theories, a second type of general theory has recently been put forward by Braithwaite (1989). He offers a general approach to crime control, arguing that the key to controlling crime is a cultural commitment to reintegrative shaming. He distinguishes between reintegrative shaming and stigmatization. According to Braithwaite, stigmatization occurs when shame is applied counterproductively and offenders are rejected from mainstream society and attracted to criminal subcultures. By contrast, reintegrative shaming means that expressions of community disapproval will be followed by gestures of re-acceptance, whereby offenders are reintegrated back into the community.

This approach has been regarded as having interesting implications for work with young offenders, but it is questionable how far the theory is sufficiently general. For example, it is difficult to imagine some violent criminals or sex offenders being welcomed back into the community. In addition, the theory is based on a particular vision of community – where a sense of community spirit and solidarity is taken as given – which may not necessarily exist.

For many theorists there is undoubtedly a tension between innovation and revisiting themes. It is easy to recognize that Braithwaite's theory of reintegrative shaming (1989) echoes many of the assumptions of labelling theory. For example, stigmatization is regarded as the result of negative labelling, while reintegrative shaming is an example of positive labelling in action. Braithwaite also draws on insights from other theoretical positions, but his own specific theory has widely been regarded as innovative and original in its own right, even if the generality of his approach is questionable. Although Braithwaite sets his work up as a general theory, in many senses it may be more useful to regard it as providing a platform for theoretical integration.

The aim of producing a general theory of crime may be a desirable goal, particularly for those who wish to make some sense of the many varied explanations of crime and criminality that exist, or simply wish to move beyond such explanations. However, it is questionable how far this goal is achievable in practice. The difficulties of producing a truly general theory are illustrated by the two examples above and have led some to suggest that theoretical integration may be a more realistic target, whereby the insights of various perspectives are drawn upon. How far the crime theorist should strive for originality or, alternatively, build on existing approaches is a difficult issue. We will consider this tension between innovation and revisiting recurring themes by exploring issues relating to theoretical integration and several current approaches influential in criminological theory.

A case for integration

Given that the numerous explanations of crime and criminality that exist are often based on different levels of explanation, it follows that certain theories will be able to explain certain issues better than others. For example, if we wanted to consider the experiences of female offenders, we would most probably be drawn in the first instance to feminist theories. By contrast, theories that focused on the layout of the social environment, such as those put forward by the Chicago School, would not be particularly helpful. Alternatively, if we wanted to focus on social class in understanding the causes of crime, our attention would most likely turn towards Marxist theories. However, individual-level explanations of crime and criminality may not be seen as helpful in this context.

Some theories will be more suited to explaining certain issues than others, but the various theoretical perspectives are not necessarily mutually exclusive. We do not have to choose just one theory that we subscribe to over all the others; it is possible to use insights from different approaches to explain different phenomena. This is exactly what theoretical integration refers to – drawing on more than one perspective.

What, then, is the point of integrating theories? For some researchers it may be desirable to overcome the weaknesses of one approach by combining it with the insights of another. Integration enables us to generate new ideas about crime and deviance as well as new research findings. Or we may wish to explore more than one aspect of the crime–criminal problem, and therefore need to draw on theories that address different levels of explanation. At a more fundamental level, there may be a desire to impose some order on criminological theory, enabling us to make sense of the existing body of knowledge, which includes so many unconnected themes and ideas.

There are various examples of theoretical integration, some more complex than others. One example that draws on just two main perspectives is Marxist feminism, which combines a Marxist analysis of social class and state power with feminist concerns regarding the experiences of women in the criminal justice system (see Rafter and Natalizia, 1981). A slightly more complex attempt at integration is offered by Braithwaite (1989), who draws on the insights of several perspectives, including labelling, social control and subcultural theories, in outlining his own original theory of reintegrative shaming.

Other theorists have gone as far as to combine what many commentators regard as rival positions. Sampson and Laub (1993) draw upon the two models of 'criminal careers' and 'criminal propensity' in their 'life-course' perspective, even though these two approaches are based on quite different assumptions. In line with the propensity model, Sampson and Laub recognize that there is continuity in anti-social and deviant behaviour throughout life and across various dimensions. However, at the same time they note that despite these continuities, attachments formed in later life, such as those to the labour force and to marriage, can alter the course of life trajectories. Attempts to chart different types of criminal career are therefore regarded as valuable.

In spite of the examples above, it is worth noting at this point that there is not actually any universal consensus over the strategy of theoretical integration in criminology. Some commentators are directly opposed to it. According to Hirschi (1979), integrated theories do not necessarily have any greater explanatory value than individual theories. In his view, the individual merits of a given theory become obscured and unclear when integrated with other approaches.

Even if we do not accept Hirschi's point about the dangers of integration (1979), it is important to be aware that we cannot necessarily integrate everything. It requires some serious thought as to which particular strands of criminological theory will be drawn upon in order to explore a certain issue. In brief, we should not just integrate for the sake of it, but only if we can show that there is some logical reason for doing so that has been rigorously thought out. Drawing on other people's work will result in recurring themes in criminology and may lead us, at times, to question whether the discipline is saying anything new. Yet, integration also has the potential to aid the development of fresh and innovative ideas, taking the discipline into unexplored territory.

Current theoretical approaches influential in criminological thinking

What theories are currently 'in', and how do they differ from what has gone before? The following section gives an indication of just some of the theoretical approaches that are receiving a considerable amount of attention at this time. Hence, these areas are focuses for debate and innovation. As should become clear, the first section below is not so much about one particular approach, but more of an introduction to a theoretical 'debate' that is of contemporary relevance.

Criminal propensity versus criminal careers

Broadly speaking, those working under the theoretical framework of criminal careers are concerned with classifying different types of offender according to various aspects of their career in crime, such as frequency of crimes committed. Recent developments within this area have increasingly revolved around the issue of age, and how far it is possible to classify offenders according to the age in which they first become involved in crime – often referred to as 'age of onset'. For example, a distinction has been made between adolescence-limited and life-course persistent offenders (Moffitt, 1993). The former group generally begin offending as adolescents and stop in early adulthood; often their crimes are regarded as symptomatic of teenage rebellion, and they may include activities such as drinking, drug-taking and joyriding. Life-course persistent offenders, on the other hand, tend to be characterized by early age of onset and offence versatility, and they are seen to be more likely to commit serious violent offences.

In contrast to the above approach, advocates of the criminal propensity position argue that there is no point in trying to distinguish between different types of offender. This is because they believe that criminality (or the propensity to commit crime) tends to be highly stable; in other words it is generally similar early and late in a person's life. Such theorists also note that criminality tends to decline uniformly for all offenders as they get older; this is attributed to a decline in their propensity to commit crime. Commentators such as Gottfredson and Hirschi (1990) are frequently associated with this theoretical position.

According to Gottfredson and Hirschi (1990), the identification of the causes of crime at one age will suffice to identify them at other ages as well. As has been previously noted, the individual-level cause of crime that they particularly focus on is low self-control. Because they hold that criminality will decline uniformly for all offenders over time, Gottfredson and Hirschi suggest that it is meaningless to talk of different stages in an individual criminal career. Therefore, criminal career terminology that talks of careers starting and persisting is regarded as redundant.

The criminal propensity and criminal career approaches are frequently set up as rival positions; however it is important to recognize that they are based on quite different assumptions. Does an individual's propensity to commit crime, which is established during early childhood, adequately explain why certain people will become offenders? Or do we require some further explanation? Moffitt's life-course persistent offender (1993) tends to exhibit fairly stable behavioural patterns throughout life, and in this respect fits well with the propensity model. Yet if we accept the existence of a certain group of individuals whose offending is adolescence-limited (that is, they stop offending after an adolescent phase), then perhaps something more than individual propensity or low self-control is required as an explanation. We have already noted that Sampson and Laub (1993) draw upon insights from both models in their life-course perspective.

Research on desistance

Desistance refers to desisting from crime, or 'going straight'. This concept is often associated with criminal career terminology; yet research on desistance is actually moving away from the original formulation of the criminal career thesis (cf. Blumstein et al., 1986) and developing as a topic in its own right. Theorizing desistance is regarded as important in enabling us to understand how and why certain types of offender stop offending.

While desistance has often been regarded as a termination event, particularly in statistical models that aim to chart different careers in crime, criminologists are increasingly recognizing that it is far more accurate to regard desistance as a process. As Liebrich (1993) rightly notes, 'going straight' is often 'curved', and certainly most individuals do not suddenly stop becoming involved in crime. Recent research in this area (e.g. Maruna, 2001) indicates that it is more productive to regard desistance as a maintenance process, something that has to be continually worked at. Therefore, rather than asking *why* individuals may give up a life of crime, it may be more useful to ask *how* they actually do it. What conditions enable an individual to successfully desist?

Research on desistance is developing quite rapidly at the moment and is an important area of study. As well as being valuable in their own right, explanations of how individuals desist from crime offer an interesting contrast to much previous research that focuses on how and why individuals become involved in crime in the first place.

Restorative justice

Restorative justice is not so much a theory as a philosophical approach. In other words, it is a set of principles and values which offer a basis on which to proceed in dispensing justice. It is included here because it gained serious momentum in criminal justice circles following the publication of Braithwaite's theory of reintegrative shaming (1989). Contemporary notions of restorative justice are based quite heavily on Braithwaite's work. Rather than focusing simply on the need to process and punish offenders – which often results in victims and others affected by crime being ignored – restorative justice aims to meet the needs of victims, communities and offenders. This approach has been influential in a number of western countries in recent years and is one of the key principles underpinning youth justice policy and practice in the UK.

One of the most established forms of restorative justice practice is victim–offender mediation, which involves victims and offenders engaging in either direct or indirect communication. Offenders are held directly accountable for their actions and are expected to consider the full consequences of what they have done. They are then given the opportunity to volunteer to make reparation. Reparation might include, for example, time spent labouring on a practical project of benefit to the victim and/or the wider community. For victims, it is felt that, among other things, participation in meaningful dialogue with offenders can reduce the fear of revictimization.

However, the criticisms previously made of Braithwaite's theory still apply. Victims who are physically and emotionally scarred may be unlikely to want any form of communication with their violent attacker. In spite of this, a restorative justice approach does have the potential to be valuable with regard to certain youth crimes, such as vandalism, graffiti and burglary, where there has not necessarily been any violence against the person. Certainly restorative justice has been high on the criminological agenda, and it is an interesting example of how theories of crime can be built upon and made valuable to criminal justice practitioners.

Criminal careers and criminal propensity models, research on desistance and a commitment to restorative justice are all particularly influential in criminology at the start of the twenty-first century. However, this is certainly not to say that the theories previously outlined have been discarded. Researchers continue to work on aspects of strain theory and labelling theory, for example, developing and building upon the original concepts and ideas. Furthermore, there is an increasing tendency among some commentators to try to integrate various perspectives.

Conclusion

This chapter has introduced a range of theories through a process of ordering ideas and posing questions. Theory has been presented as a means of explaining complex criminological phenomena. While theory can be viewed as social commentary tied to moments in time, it can also represent longer-term projects rather than short-term responses to social issues. Explanations tend to be partial, concerned with specific and limited aspects of criminality, but represent in-depth analyses of the available evidence.

We have outlined some key moments in the history of criminological ideas, noting that these can be understood as responses to particular questions. We have also shown that there are certain questions that we can ask ourselves when trying to evaluate particular theoretical positions. These questions can help us to assess both the merits and weaknesses of particular approaches.

There has also been a concern to show that theorizing is about real people in the real world trying to make sense of the times in which they live. This raises questions about how applicable to social problems explanations of crime might actually be. In chapter 6 we consider the difficult issue of how far theories of crime and criminality can actually be applied in practice, with particular reference to influencing social policy.

6

Criminology and Social Policy

How does an applied subject like criminology link to the public arena of social policy and its construction? By exploring the criminologist's role and how policy is developed, this chapter illustrates ways of assessing criminology's impact. We question how long-standing tensions, between 'administrative research' and criminology as 'social commentary', will adapt in a changing research environment.

This chapter asks what is the point of theory and research for an applied discipline like criminology? Criminology is concerned with the needs of real people in the real world, whether they are victims, offenders, agents of criminal justice or the wider community. If they are to have any influence at all on policy and practice, theories and ideas about crime and deviance need to be disseminated both within and outside the academic environment. To ask criminologists to influence public debate and the construction of policy is a tough requirement and, sadly, criminology often fails to deliver. However, one needs to recognize that the task is not a simple one.

Understanding the link between theory and policy is difficult and so needs to be accomplished in stages. Initially, it requires unravelling naive conceptualizations of how researchers work and requires some awareness of how social policy is developed and implemented. In understanding both these processes, one can then go on to assess how much impact criminology has made on the public arena and the ways in which it has failed as an *applied* discipline.

Democratic societies are fuelled by both compromise and conflict, and social policy is the focus of debate between competing ideologies. Criminologists compete with other powerful voices for the attention of policy-makers. Policy itself, expressed through legislation and funding initiatives, is subject to change, considered amendment and unintended outcomes. To explore in greater depth how criminological theory and research links with this arena of policy formation, we return to a discussion of the role of criminologists themselves. In chapter 1 a fundamental divide was described between 'administrative research' and what, in chapter 5, we have broadly described as social commentary. Like all schisms, it is exaggerated; nonetheless it is one that is alive and well in modern criminology and salient to understanding and assessing the uses of criminology.

The role of the criminologist

Criminological work does not take place in a social, academic or financial vacuum. Criminologists can fundamentally alter the way we think about crime and what to do about it. Labelling theorists really did make policy-makers begin to question the value of locking people up and, indeed, this approach remains a challenge to the massive prison-building programme that features in the spending plans of many governments. Criminologists making such fundamental challenges tend to be on the outside of government, usually working in university departments or in pressure groups attempting to alter policy in a significant way. Criminologists can also generate new evidence and develop innovative ways of both accessing and analysing large-scale research data. Both routes are expensive in time, money and personnel.

Since the 1950s the Home Office and other governmental agencies have employed quite considerable numbers of criminologists. In fact, the Home Office is the largest single employer of criminological researchers in the UK (Morgan, 2000). Rod Morgan, now chief inspector of probation but formerly an academic, has recently made the criticism that Home Office-funded research tends to be completely atheoretical, and purely about the gathering of so-called 'facts'. In other words, there is no attempt to see the wider picture. In contrast, a criminologist such as Stan Cohen (see 'Denial as a crime' in chapter 7) would see such a wider social commentary as a central task for criminology, including recognition of the moral and political implications of government initiatives.

Hence, Home Office work in the 1990s turned to evaluation of governmental initiatives, such as the crime reduction programme. Home Office criminologists may not actually do the work themselves but they supervise contracts handed out to university departments. The aim of such work is usually to consider whether – or to what extent – these governmental initiatives are actually working. Evaluation studies developed in this way tend to accept the basic premise or framework of government policy. So, for example, an evaluation of the introduction of closed circuit television (CCTV) monitoring would try to measure its effectiveness, but would not try to challenge the wisdom of developing this kind of surveillance within a liberal democracy.

Thus the two strands of criminology – social commentary and administrative – that we have emphasized in earlier chapters (see especially chapters 1 and 5) are both alive and very relevant in the consideration of the links between theory and practice in criminology.

For researchers hoping to undertake new projects, funding is clearly a very important issue. Lack of funding creates serious problems for potential researchers, and for those engaged in large-scale evidence-based work, research without funding is impossible. Many of the funding opportunities that do exist are provided by central government and so will reflect their interests and concerns to a certain degree. This is regarded by some as a fundamental limitation of social research in this area.

For example, Booth (1988) notes that policy-makers tend to draw their values from the prevailing hierarchy of power, whereas within the social sciences there is a strong identification with the underdog, the powerless and the outsider. However, researchers negotiating research grants are under increasing pressure to demonstrate that their research is policy-relevant. As Finch (1986) notes, that the research has a social policy focus does not mean that the results will be of poor quality. Yet for many social scientists, policy-oriented research is seen as turning the researcher into a kind of spy in the service of the ruling class.

Our position is that criminological researchers should always consider the practical and policy implications of their work, but with a view to *questioning* rather than *reinforcing* government ideology. Yet even a questioning approach is not always possible, and this puts in jeopardy the criminologist's role as social commentator. Given that the Home Office is a government agency, working in the interests of the government of the day, many criminologists may find themselves uncertain about how impartial and objective their Home Office-funded research can truly be.

Morgan notes that it is widely contended that most Home Office-funded research tends to be, among other things, both short-termist and uncritical. It is short-termist in the sense that it is often designed to assess whether whatever is being evaluated is having an immediate impact. Meanwhile, it is 'uncritical, in the sense that it does not question general government policy but merely reports whether the evidence collected supports the continuation of one policy tactic as opposed to another' (Morgan, 2000: 72).

In spite of these criticisms, Morgan also describes how Home Office research has an international reputation for being methodologically demanding and professionally competent. In addition, the Home Office has been largely responsible for amassing a wealth of empirical research findings. This represents a very rich source of data that criminologists can draw upon.

Certainly, the fact that a great deal of criminological research is funded by government is not something peculiar to the UK. At the American Society of Criminology's annual conference in 2000, William Chambliss (2000) argued that it was 'a tragedy' that the Department of Justice in America controls the discipline of criminology and all of its funding. Like the Home Office in England, the Department of Justice inevitably has an agenda that it wants to promote.

Another important port of call for potential criminological researchers in the UK is the Economic and Social Research Council (ESRC). This is an independent organization, although it receives much of its own funding from the government. The ESRC does not deal specifically with criminology but funds a broad range of social research. A great deal of criminological research fits within the ESRC's list of thematic priorities. For those not wishing to directly address policy-related issues, the ESRC is a particularly important organization.

Other research funds may also be available from charitable foundations, such as the Nuffield Foundation, the Joseph Rowntree Foundation and the Leverhulme Trust. Some researchers may actively seek out funds from these organizations, particularly if they want to criticize government policy and practice. This kind of research may then be used to assist pressure groups and voluntary organizations in the pursuit of their particular policy preferences.

BOX 6.1   ASSESSING THE SOCIAL IMPLICATIONS OF CRIMINOLOGY

When reading about a theory or a piece of research, ask yourself these questions:

1   What is the theory or research broadly concerned with – crime, criminal behaviour, the criminal justice system?
2   As a result of the work, who or what may be required to change – individuals, groups, institutions, society?
3   What implications for policy and practice might there be at the following levels?

 • local
 • national
 • international

4   Does the theory support the status quo, or challenge the existing social order?

For example, researcher Barry Goldson collaborated with The Children's Society, a leading children's charity in the UK, to produce a research report on contemporary responses to youth crime (Goldson and Peters, 2000). The report is highly critical of government policy, and it argues that current measures for dealing with young offenders are too harsh and have harmful consequences for many children. However, it is important to point out that, like the Home Office, the voluntary organizations also have their own particular agendas that they wish to promote. Such organizations may be fiercely censorious of research findings that do not support their own policies and practice.

Although very different, the two strands of 'administrative research' and criminology as 'social commentary' are essential parts of the jigsaw. To understand how a particular piece of criminological work might interact with the sphere of social policy, then, always requires further questioning and evaluation (see box 6.1). It also needs more awareness of what 'social policy' might mean in practice, and we now turn to the process by which policy is constructed.

Crime and social policy

In contemporary society it needs to be recognized that a great deal of what we call 'crime' and 'criminalization' is discussed in the political arena and is set up as a social problem that needs to be dealt with. This leads to the implicit assumption that the problem of crime can be solved. Politicians, academics and criminal justice agents are all in the business of searching for solutions to the problem of crime.

The development and introduction of new policies and legislation is one of the key ways in which potential solutions can be implemented. For example, if we believe that harsher punishments would lead to a reduction in certain types of crime, we may wish to see a policy that allows for longer prison sentences. Equally, if we feel that prison does more harm than good to many offenders, we may be committed to a policy of increased community-based sentences. Criminologists are involved in this kind of policy question in various ways – such as investigating whether harsher punishments do, indeed, lead to a reduction in certain types of crime or by highlighting the dangers of imprisoning people unnecessarily.

Policy can be defined as a set of ideas and proposals for action which result in a government decision. Theories and ideas are absolutely crucial in enabling us to make sense of various aspects of crime and criminality. Yet it is often research evidence rather than pure theory that tends to be emphasized when new legislation is justified by ministers, regardless of whether or not the research was conducted within a strong theoretical framework.

While research can be useful to policy-makers who wish to justify a new piece of legislation, it is important to note that it is just one of several factors that may influence the policy-making process. As we saw in chapter 2, researchers represent just one source of policy advice and one source of knowledge about crime. Other policy initiators include: the mass media, the general public, think-tanks, pressure groups, voluntary organizations, policy units and select committees. Research that is not used by government is not redundant, as research results can be disseminated among criminal justice professionals, thereby encouraging wider debate and awareness. Results may be picked up by the media or used by a pressure group to lobby government. The time may not be ripe for direct governmental action but the research may be put to use on a future occasion; however, the criminologist as 'social commentator' can influence the development

Figure 6.1 Tributaries to legislation, 1987–1991
Source: Lord Windlesham, *Responses to Crime, Volume 2: Penal Policy in the Making* (Oxford: Clarendon, 1993)

of the debate between potential 'policy initiators'. To understand how this might be, we need to understand more about how criminal justice policy develops and results in legislation.

The development of criminal justice policy and legislation

Policies and legislation aimed at dealing with crime are a central feature of British political life. Windlesham (1993) notes that between 1948 and 1991 Parliament passed eight substantive Criminal Justice Acts for England and Wales, plus a Criminal Law Act and four Scottish Criminal Justice Acts. In addition, several acts dealing with criminal justice administration, international co-operation and various other minor matters were introduced.

Since 1993, when Windlesham was writing, issues of law and order have remained very high on the political agenda. In the UK, the New Labour government's pledge to be 'tough on crime, tough on the causes of crime' became something of a national catchphrase.

Windlesham provides us with a useful discussion of how penal policy is developed and enacted in legislation. As a former Home Office minister, who then became chairman of the Parole Board and eventually president of Victim Support, he has much first-hand experience. Although focusing primarily on legislation enacted between 1987 and 1991 (and specifically the Criminal Justice Act 1991), Windlesham produced a chart that provides a way of looking at the issues. He describes the sources of legislation as the various tributaries which flow into the river that ultimately leads into the 'Sea of Statutes' (see figure 6.1).

Let us consider some of the ingredients that eventually move the flow of the river towards the 'Sea of Statutes'. Firstly, there is 'penal reform' placed fairly near the top of the diagram. This represents the efforts of organizations like the Howard League of Penal Reform and the National Association for the Care and Resettlement of Offenders (NACRO) to get issues on to the political agenda. Penal reform groups put pressure on the government of the day, aiming to improve the treatment of offenders. Such groups were particularly instrumental in campaigning for the abolition of the death penalty, which was finally abolished in the UK in 1969.

Of course, some of the ideas put forward by penal reform groups do not get very far because, as we said earlier, the time may not be ripe for a particular change. It is noteworthy that the Howard Association (as the Howard League was formerly known) had been campaigning for the abolition of capital punishment since the 1870s. In figure 6.1 Windlesham is showing the efforts that are successful and, in doing so, overlooks the fact that much of the work of reform groups may not be taken up.

Moving down towards the middle of the diagram, note the set of hazardous mountain ranges to be conquered before legislation gets onto the statute book. The mountain range can be usefully identified as 'financial constraints', which in the last two decades have been the hazards of efficiency and effectiveness along with the spectre of cash limits.

However, there are also other issues to consider. For example, on the right-hand side of the diagram there are some strong currents being generated from the high mountain range of 'political conviction'. This refers to political beliefs and opinions. The government of the day are inevitably guided by their own political ideology and beliefs which will be strong driving forces in the policy-making process. Hence 'political conviction' appears as such a high mountain range. Mountains, of course, may not only block the flow of the river, but the falling height may also encourage a faster flow. Since the Second World War 'political conviction' has often been buttressed by a range of mountains called 'American example', where what happens in America is subsequently influential in the UK.

Windlesham's map is helpful but not definitive. What he perhaps overlooks is the other small mountain range called 'continental shelf' that buttresses the 'penal reform' range, for some reformers have been much more impressed by what can be learnt from continental Europe than from America. However, the general idea is that all these various tributaries flow into a river which is continually moving, sometimes slowly and sometimes quite fast, towards the 'Sea of Statutes'.

Windlesham characterizes 'research' as an ominously black-looking cloud at the top of the diagram. The water from a cloudburst may dampen enthusiasm, but it can also be used to help increase the flow of the river towards the 'Sea of Statutes'. Notably absent from the diagram is 'criminological theory'. 'Criminological theory' may inform the cloud of research but, as has already been noted, not all research is theoretically informed.

In some ways 'criminological theory' can be regarded as all-pervasive. Indeed, there are some implicit criminological theories that inform conviction politics and penal reform as much as they do academic research. For example, encouraging the 'responsibility of parents' occurs, in part, because it is thought that parents exercising responsibility are important in the fight against crime.

Yet, suggesting that theory is 'all-pervasive', like air, may be misleading, as there are a whole variety of criminological theories, both implicit and explicit, that are around at any given time. Perhaps theories are more like a series of smells. Some of the smells regarded as 'fragrant' in the hills of 'penal reform' may be regarded as 'pungent' by people living on the hills of 'political conviction'. There is a danger in pushing the analogy too far, but theory may not always be easy to sense, like air or smells in the air, when we ask how criminological theories are relevant to legislation. It is possible to recognize tacit theorizing underpinning both popular opinion and media representations of crime.

Interestingly, Windlesham does not include public opinion or the mass media in his diagram. Yet the media perhaps play their most important role in shaping and reflecting aspects of public opinion and in helping to determine whether the time is ripe for social change in the first place. This is not to say that we all passively accept what we read in the press and hear on the news, but media consumption is such an entrenched part of our daily lives that sometimes we may be scarcely aware of the influence it can have upon us.

Abercrombie et al. (2000) note that some 98 per cent of households in Britain own at least one television set, and 53 per cent own two or more. On average, each member of the population watches about twenty-five hours of television a week. Meanwhile, 26 million people in Britain read a national daily newspaper. The biggest selling newspaper is the *Sun*, which had a readership of 9.9 million people in 1997 (Abercrombie et al., 2000).

By selecting particular issues and events that are regarded as significant, and therefore newsworthy, the media exercises a great deal of power in establishing a social agenda. Indeed, the British press have been known to amplify social problems beyond their real significance, thereby contributing to a national 'moral panic' (see Cohen, 1973). The extensive media coverage surrounding the murder of James Bulger in England in 1993, by two 10-year-old boys, is a case in point. Some commentators have noted that, despite the young age of the killers, the tone of much of the media coverage was harshly punitive. This contributed to growing public fears about youth crime and the further demonization of young people, whereby children were increasingly regarded as capable of 'evil' (Newburn, 1997).

In terms of having an impact on society, one of the major advantages that the media has over research is that it generally reaches a much wider audience. Having said this, the media can aid researchers by providing them with an audience, too. Criminologists occasionally appear on the broadcast media and increasingly have their ideas published in the written media. Therefore, an opportunity of sorts does exist for researchers to use the media as a route to engaging in the wider social policy debate.

The influence of research

So far we have noted that academics and researchers represent just one source of policy advice. Sometimes they find themselves competing against the tide of public opinion, which may be heavily influenced by the media, in order to get certain issues on to the social and political agenda. In Windlesham's diagram (figure 6.1) research is portrayed as a cloud that may dampen enthusiasm for a particular policy or provide further support for it.

Yet, occasionally, research has had a more direct influence on government thinking than this picture allows for. In particular, by increasing social awareness of issues and questioning entrenched views, research has contributed directly to changes in social policy. The following two examples represent the different ways in which research and criminological theory can interact with the construction of policy-making. Interaction between legislation and ideas occurs over long periods of time, as well as in response to immediate and specific information, and the first example, concerning the use of mental hospitals and prisons, illustrates the ebb and flow of one idea over a long period of time.

Tearing prisons down and building prisons up

Since the 1970s there has been much focus on the possibilities of decarceration and deinstitutionalization. These terms are a shorthand for the policy of closing down asylums, prisons and reformatories of various kinds and replacing them with a range of facilities that will allow mental patients, prisoners and young offenders to be supported in the community. This movement towards community care stemmed directly from the work of criminologists and others (Goffman, 1968a, 1968b; Laing and Esterson, 1973; Szasz, 1961; Thorpe et al., 1980) demonstrating both in theory and in practice that placing people in institutions could have bad effects that actually made the situation worse. Being taken away from their family and losing their jobs helped to create a 'downward spiral' when people were put in institutions; the stigma of being an ex-prisoner made finding a job more difficult and led to a set of new problems on being released, problems that Lemert (1967) characterized as 'secondary deviance'. Of course, the recognition of all this is not entirely new. So, for instance, the report from the departmental committee on prisons (1895), known as the Gladstone Committee, recognized the dangers of 'contamination' – that is, those going into prison for the first time learned bad habits from more persistent offenders, known as recidivists. Hence, the Gladstone Report successfully recommended the separation of those in prison for the first time (the 'stars') from the others (the 'ordinaries'). The more recent 'care in the community' movement – based on work by social scientists – was, however, saying much more and highlighting the dangers and damaging effects of entering any institution.

In the 1980s there was a largely bipartisan approach in Parliament, with both major political parties accepting the overall aim of either closing down psychiatric institutions or trying to reduce the prison population. The various community control schemes for criminals can easily be presented as enlightened reforms, but deinstitionalization programmes may also be enthusiastically embraced by governments as they recognize that they may be a cheaper as well as a more effective alternative (Abercrombie et al., 2000). However, since the late 1980s, the risk that some mentally disturbed people represent to the wider community, together with the dangers stemming from some offenders such as paedophiles, has become a major public policy issue. Furthermore, in an attempt to bring down the crime rates, there was a brief period in the 1990s when the notion that 'prison works' was embraced by the then Conservative government. The Labour government, in its second term of office (2001 onwards), undertook an evidence-based crime-reduction programme while maintaining an extensive prison-building programme.

Burglary in a Dwelling

Mike Maguire's research *Burglary in a Dwelling* was published in 1982. Up to this time there had been no data gathered specifically on burglary victims in England. Maguire's work aimed to illuminate aspects of the offence of burglary, as well as the experience of the offender and the victim (see box 6.2). Yet it was the chapter on victims that really attracted attention. As a result, Maguire became one of the very few British experts on victims (Rock, 1990).

BOX 6.2   BURGLARY IN A DWELLING

Maguire demonstrated that burglary in a dwelling resulted in much more than a material loss, and actually had a severe emotional impact on many victims:

> The idea of a criminal penetrating one of the most private places of a person's world – his or her own home – is unpleasant and upsetting, and can produce psychological effects which last long beyond the loss or inconvenience suffered at the time. (1982: 1)

Maguire found that 83 per cent of the burglary victims in his study had experienced strong reactions on discovering that their home had been burgled. Meanwhile, 65 per cent were still aware of some continuing impact on their lives between four and ten weeks later. When asked about the worst aspect of being burgled, only 32 per cent of victims spoke of loss or damage. Meanwhile, 41 per cent cited feelings of intrusion, and 19 per cent of emotional upset.

Source: Adapted from M. Maguire, *Burglary in a Dwelling* (London: Heinemann, 1982)

Interestingly, prior to the publication of Maguire's work, Home Office research had played down the experience of victimization. For example, Paul Rock notes that when the idea for the British Crime Survey was first put forward at a conference organized by the Home Office, none of the members of the National Association of Victim Support Schemes was invited to attend. According to Rock: 'it was therefore made abundantly clear that crime surveys were not supposed to illuminate the character of victims or the experience of crime. They were instead taken to be a method of improving what was called the "criminal justice data base"' (1995: 13).

The first British Crime Survey was undertaken in 1982, the same year in which Maguire's work appeared. Given that the Home Office had funded Maguire's research, and burglary in a dwelling was in fact one of the most common serious offences recorded by the police at this time, they were unable to ignore the significance of his research findings on victims. The second British Crime Survey in 1984 included questions on the emotional impact of crime upon victims. In 'Taking account of crime: key findings from the 1984 British Crime Survey' (1985), Hough and Mayhew note in their acknowledgements that 'Mike Maguire of the Centre for Criminological Research, Oxford, took the lead in designing questionnaire items on victim support schemes' (p. iv). Hence, Maguire's work resulted in the Home Office having a complete change of heart about the importance of victims in the British Crime Survey.

The Home Office was also influenced by Joanna Shapland's research (1982) on victims in the criminal justice system, which drew attention to victims' dissatisfaction with the criminal justice process. Victim support was subsequently placed firmly on the political agenda when the Home Affairs Committee reported on victim issues in 1984. The committee's report, *Compensation and Support for Victims of Crime*, stated that 'some of the shortcomings in the provision of facilities for the victims of crime have been brought to notice in two useful research studies carried out by Dr Joanna Shapland' (1984: 1). Short summaries of both of Shapland's research studies were included in the committee's report, which went on to recommend that arrangements should be made by the Probation Service to set up the necessary infrastructure for local victim support schemes. In addition, the committee proposed that the Home Office should be prepared to meet the additional expenditure incurred. In 1986 the Home Office agreed to fund local victim support schemes.

The above examples indicate how crime research can help to trigger policy reforms by identifying social problems. Furthermore, a great deal of research is increasingly conducted in order to evaluate the effectiveness of new legislation. Following the impact of the research on burglary in a dwelling, Mike Maguire and a colleague were subsequently commissioned by the Home Office to conduct some evaluation research on victim support schemes (see Maguire and Corbett, 1987).

Does social policy deliver?

Much of this chapter has been devoted to looking at the various ways in which research may influence social change, with particular reference to the development of policy and, hence, subsequent social legislation. In chapter 5, we met the idea of criminologists as social commentators, and in this section we explore the importance of that role by questioning social policy itself. We ask if commentary on governmental action is merely indulgence, or does it have a constructive role to play? Policy, it must be remembered, impacts upon people's lives – and most profoundly on the lives of the most vulnerable. For social change to occur, new policies need to work in practice. Yet some policies are unclear, contradictory and confusing. For policies to work, they need to be implemented properly, translated into coherent laws and practices and supported by the proper allocation of funds.

Hence, influencing change in social policy and through subsequent legislation is not the end of the story. Social change does not occur when a minister introduces a radical new policy. Criminological commentaries, then, are part of an iterative, dynamic political process that does not assume all legislation to be the acme of achievement. Change occurs when that policy is actually implemented and its effects shape people's lives. Whatever the original intentions, some of those effects may be unplanned, accidental, contradictory or – indeed – undesirable.

Criminology as 'social commentary' can provide a detailed analysis of policy development, decisions, implementation and outcomes. Rather than criticism for the sake of criticism, it can provide rigorous questioning and identification of achievements and failures in policy outcomes, as well as set the agenda for future action. As an example of this process of policy evaluation, we now examine the area of youth policy. It will become clear that there is a lack of coherence both *within* specific measures and *between* policies affecting children and young people, and that there remain problems with attempts to introduce 'joined-up policy'.

Youth policy: failure of delivery

The Children Act 1989 was a fairly comprehensive piece of legislation that dealt with issues such as child protection, parental responsibility and provision for children who are unable to live at home. The child welfare provisions outlined in this Act were the subject of broad political consensus in Parliament; yet how far they have delivered in practice is a matter of some debate.

Particular criticisms of the 1989 Act have focused quite extensively on the lack of support provided for young people leaving the care system. Traditionally, many young people have been required to leave care at age 16, often finding themselves with nowhere to live, no money and nobody to depend on. Under section 24 of the Act, local authorities have the 'power to assist' care-leavers up until the age of 21, yet research has consistently shown that many care-leavers have received very little help (e.g. Broad, 1998). Because the 'power to assist' is not an actual 'duty', it has been left open to the interpretation of individual social services departments. The result has been the uneven development of local authority leaving-care services.

In comparison to their peers, care-leavers as a group are disproportionately more likely to end up in the prison population. The lack of support that many have received upon reaching the age of 16 has been put forward as one possible reason for this. However, it has often been the case that local authorities have not been provided with adequate funds for care-leavers. Sir William Utting notes that: 'the resources available for the Act have been unreasonably constrained, not only by the general squeeze on local authority spending, but also by the effects within social services of the government's failure to make proper provision for its policies of community care' (1999: 35).

Here, then, we have an example of a policy for care-leavers that looked good on paper but was never fully successful in practice, partly because government failed to provide local authorities with appropriate funds. It is noteworthy that section 24 of the 1989 Act has recently been amended by the new Children (Leaving Care) Act 2000, which was implemented from October 2001. In recognition of the difficulties faced by young people leaving the care system, this latest Act places new 'duties' on local authorities to provide support and accommodation.

Youth policy: interactive contradictions

Policies that may seem reasonable when considered independently can, alongside each other, introduce *interactive* contradictions. According to Jones and Bell (2000), current policy constructions of childhood, youth and adulthood are varied and confused. They focus particularly on the difficulties of balancing youth dependency with parental responsibility.

Under the Crime and Disorder Act 1998, children as young as 10 years old are regarded as criminally responsible – capable of appreciating the moral significance of their actions in the same way as an

---

BOX 6.3   SOME AGES IN LEGISLATION

Age   Rights/responsibilities acquired

8   Criminal responsibility (Scotland)

10   Criminal responsibility (England and Wales)

13   Child employment

16   Can leave school
      Can contribute to National Insurance and pay income tax
      Age of heterosexual consent
      Can marry with parents' consent in England and Wales
      (without consent in Scotland)

17   Can drive a car

18   Age of majority
      Can marry without parents' consent in England and
      Wales
      Current age of consent among male homosexuals
      Can vote
      Can sign tenancy (16 in Scotland)
      Can buy alcoholic beverages
      Can claim National Insurance (including unemployment
      benefit)
      Can claim social security (at 18–21 rate)

21   Previous age of majority

22   Adult minimum wage rate

25   Adult levels of income support and housing benefit

Source: G. Jones and R. Bell, *Balancing Acts: Youth, Parenting and Public Policy* (York: York Publishing Services/Joseph Rowntree Foundation, 2000)

---

adult (see box 6.3). (In Scotland, the age of criminal responsibility is set at the even lower age of 8.) Yet, according to the Children Act 1989 and the United Nations Convention on the Rights of the Child, a child is a person below the age of 18. This is just one status ambiguity created by policies affecting children and young people.

As Jones and Bell (2000) demonstrate, while a person can seek employment at age 13, and contribute to National Insurance and pay income tax at age 16, they are not eligible for the adult minimum wage until they are 22. In addition, they are not eligible for adult levels of income support and housing benefit until they are 25. It is clear that different policies define youth in different ways, and this can lead to some confusion.

Jones and Bell further note that many current policies are based on a dependency assumption, whereby young people constructed as economically dependent can turn to their parents for further financial support. For example, this assumption is evident in the continued means-testing of parents for university tuition fees.

At the same time, many policies are based on a parenting assumption, that parents are willing and able to provide extended support to their children. Clearly this may not be the case for low-income families. The problem is that policies that imply that young people are dependent in some way are not balanced by policies that define parental responsibility. This puts some young people at risk of social exclusion.

Joined-up youth policy

Tackling social exclusion was one of the British Labour government's key concerns after taking power in 1997. Since then there has been an emphasis on creating 'joined-up' solutions to what is essentially regarded as a joined-up problem – with the potential for eliminating some of the policy contradictions described above.

> The 'joined-up nature of social problems is one of the key factors underlying the concept of social exclusion. . . . It includes low income, but is broader and focuses on the link between problems such as, for example, unemployment, poor skills, high crime, poor housing and family breakdown. Only when these links are properly understood and addressed will policies really be effective. (Social Exclusion Unit, 2001)

The Labour government has acknowledged the need for coherence between related policies; yet, returning to our theme of youth policy, contradictions are particularly apparent in policies regarding the welfare and punishment of young people.

One of New Labour's innovative early intervention schemes forms part of the Home Office crime reduction initiative. *On Track* is a long-term programme aimed at children at risk of getting involved in crime (the intention being to improve outcomes for children at risk of social exclusion). It aims to improve inter-agency co-operation so that children at risk of offending are identified early, and they and their families are provided with consistent services during the child's development. In addition to early intervention, the government is also concerned with reintegrating back into the community those who may have become excluded. For example, the referral order introduced under the Youth Justice and Criminal Evidence Act 1999 enables offenders to make amends for their behaviour to victims and/or the wider community.

Yet other measures introduced under the Crime and Disorder Act are much more punitive in nature. We are now locking up younger and younger children (Goldson and Peters, 2000), despite the fact that the links between disadvantage and offending are well documented. It is reasonable to assume that many juvenile offenders are also children in need, who may be vulnerable in some way. Yet once children have committed an offence, under youth justice legislation they are treated first and foremost as an offender. The government states that they are 'determined to reduce the seriousness and frequency of offending by children and young people and the need for custodial sentences' (Children and Young Persons Unit, 2001: 15). At the same time, they are intending to fund an additional 2,660 prison places, which includes 400 new secure training centre places for young people in custody (Home Office, 2001).

The problem is not only that a prison sentence is stigmatizing for young people, and can lead to future social isolation and exclusion, but also that many individuals will re-offend after release. Thus, many of the more punitive measures in current youth justice legislation have the potential to seriously undermine the government's wider concern with tackling social exclusion. In this sense, New Labour's approach may be less joined up than we are led to believe.

Conclusion

Exploring criminology as an applied subject has, then, opened up a range of complex ideas. From the funding of research to the fallibility of social policy, we can see that the public arena in which the debate about crime takes place is dynamic and constantly changing. There are powerful and competing voices attempting to influence government decisions, and criminologists are but one section of society.

So does research and theory in criminology deliver as an applied discipline in the arena of social policy? To summarize the discussion so far, we have noted that research has the potential to contribute to policy in two distinct ways.

- By identifying social problems, and increasing awareness about certain issues, research can directly influence government ideology and help to trigger change in social policy (e.g. Maguire, 1982).
- Research can be used in order to assess the impact of policies and reforms that are already in place (e.g. Maguire and Corbett, 1987). Indeed, evaluations of government-funded initiatives are increasingly required.

Broadly, the two strands of 'research as social commentary' and 'administrative research' reflect a long-standing division in criminology about the purposes and funding of research (see chapter 1). In addition, they reflect different beliefs about *how* criminology should be applied to real world issues, rather than *whether* it should be applied. In addition, methods by which analysis of large-scale, public data can be developed and new data generated about criminological phenomena may be neither evaluative nor a trigger for social change. There is always a danger that research evidence is used inappropriately by ministers in order to justify their proposals. It is also entirely possible that research results may be misinterpreted, and used accordingly, by a range of other influential voices – the media, lobbyists or campaigners.

As social commentary, research and academic writing can be the source of a more serious challenge to current government policy. Such criminologists will tend to be more revered in the academic community than in government circles, where challenge is traditionally taken to be a political threat rather than an opportunity to reconsider policy. Detailed social analysis and scholarship, at its best, explores the historical and ideological underpinnings of governmental decisions, the implementation of policy and its outcomes – intended or otherwise. Of course, social commentary is not directed solely at government action; however, government is at the heart of the power that directs social policy and, hence, drives subsequent social change.

There is, however, a danger of inheriting a 1960s debate in a simplified way, typifying administrative research as unthinking endorsement of government policy while assuming that all social commentary

BOX 6.4 CAN CRIMINOLOGY DELIVER?

With the increased resources available for research and development, do we have available in this country the research and development infrastructure to manage such a large-scale research programme? 'My worry is not whether we could develop it, but whether we can develop it quickly enough.'

Do we have a skills shortage in criminological research in this country? 'I am also concerned whether British criminology has sufficiently developed the skills of numerical analysis.'

While criminology started life as a multi-disciplinary area of study, we have more recently seen the emergence of people for whom criminology is *their* discipline. The problem with this is that not all the research we are interested in necessarily fits within the existing boundaries of criminology. Can we construct the kind of multi-disciplinary teams that we are going to need to complete much of the new research agenda?

Having tried to create a better link between research, policy development and implementation at government level, do we have the necessary methodologies to blend programme development and evaluation into a single process?

While we have a reasonable research base on which to develop polices, we do not have an equally good research base on how to deliver programmes. We need to have an understanding of what hinders and what helps policy delivery.

Are our traditional disciplines and the way they are defined adequate to the new tasks of a rapidly changing social world, or do they instead reflect the organized intellectual attempt to solve yesterday's problems? Are universities flexible enough to deliver this new agenda?

At the end of the day social policy is not just about efficacy, nor is it just about efficiency. It is also about what kind of vision of civic society we are trying to achieve. In other words, it has moral purpose as well as technical purpose. Criminology needs to be able to deliver criminological wisdom and not just criminological knowledge.

Source: Adapted from a speech given by Paul Wiles, Director of Research Development and Statistics at the Home Office at the Centre for Crime and Justice Studies and the Institute for the Scientific Treatment of Delinquency, 17 November 1999

reflects insight and integrity on the part of the commentator. The proper administration of justice is an appropriate focus for criminological research, but it is not the whole of the subject. Social commentary is an essential ingredient of scholarship in an applied subject, but is not the whole of what research can encompass in criminology. This chapter has specifically looked at relationships between criminology and social policy, not at the wider impact criminology can make, for example, through the media. In addition, criminology clearly has a direct message for professionals, such as probation officers, working in the justice system.

Meanwhile, the world changes around criminology and old debates are revisited in a new environment. Not least, changes in the Home Office, the employer of the greatest numbers of criminologists, impact on this debate. The work of Research Development and Statistics (RDS) at the Home Office is to provide information that helps ministers and policy-makers take evidence-based decisions, and also helps the police, the Probation Service, the courts, immigration officials and firefighters to do their jobs as effectively as possible. Currently its work is undergoing both a renaissance and an expansion. The Labour government came into power (1997) committing itself to an evidence-led crime reduction strategy. Prime Minister Tony Blair made clear his desire to modernize the Civil Service in order to make it accountable in terms of the outcomes it delivers rather than of the outputs it produces. So, for example, the passing of a piece of legislation is not in itself a sign of success; success depends on whether the legislation achieves the changes in the real world that it was designed to produce.

Paul Wiles, director of the RDS at the Home Office, has raised some concerns as to whether criminology can respond to the opportunities provided by the twin themes of knowledge-based policy and the modernization of the Civil Service (see box 6.4). Many of his concerns directly relate to the division of skills, thinking and beliefs that are reflected in the tension between the place of administrative research and social commentary in criminology.

The drafting of policy and, to an extent, the planning of research require definitions of crime and criminality to be made. While administrative research needs agreement about how we construct social and crime issues, social commentary reflects upon some of the taken-for-granted thinking around behaviour that contravenes existing legislation. In chapters 7 and 8 we begin to blur some of the boundaries that we have, ourselves, already set up.

7

Blurring the Boundaries: Power, Protest and Pleasure

In this chapter we begin to blur the boundaries of what constitutes crime and criminal behaviour. The difficulty of defining crime is illustrated by exploring three important dilemmas – the policing of the powerful, the policing of protest and the policing of pleasure. By introducing some complexity into the concept of crime, we encourage readers to question their own taken-for-granted assumptions.

By the time most people reach chapter 7 of an introductory criminology text, it is generally assumed that readers know broadly what crime is about. We all know what crime is and can identify criminal behaviour as and when we come across it. Crime is a 'bad thing' and we want to get rid of it. This seems to be a fairly reasonable assumption. Or is it? Do we really know exactly what crime is? Is it always 'bad'? In this chapter we begin to distinguish between what we know and what we think we know about the rather elusive concept that we call crime.

So far we have treated the concept of crime as largely unproblematic – a taken-for-granted phenomenon that requires no definition. Yet, in reality, this concept is not quite so clear-cut. There are three areas that illustrate some of the dilemmas that we need to confront:

- How do we control those who make the laws?
- What do we do about those who do not like the laws?
- Why is that so many laws seem to stop us doing the things we like?

So, the three p's we need to confront are: the policing of the *powerful*; the policing of *protest;* and the policing of *pleasure.* But first, to help make sense of these three areas we turn to the most mysterious of the Greek philosophers – Socrates. He wrote nothing, preferring to pursue his ideas through public debate, but despite this lack of documentation, Socrates' work has survived to exert a powerful influence over his successors. In particular, the work of Plato and Aristotle is greatly indebted to him (Oliver, 1998). We look to Socrates to help us explore whether or not crime is always 'a bad thing' and to Durkheim to consider the social functions of crime.

Socrates facing a death sentence

We have already hinted that we may not always be comfortable with condemning criminals. In chapter 4 we mentioned how Rabbi Hugo Gryn and the publisher Robert Maxwell were subject to the 'Jew Laws' in Hungary which made criminal status hard to avoid. Socrates provides another example.

Socrates – sometimes called 'the saint and martyr of philosophy' (Gottlieb, 2000) – was sentenced to death in 399 BC by Athenian judges after a jury found him guilty of challenging the received doctrines of Athens. His prosecutors said of him: 'Socrates is an evil-doer and a curious person, searching into things under the earth and above the heaven; and making the worse appear the better, and teaching all this to others' (Oliver, 1998: 16). You can imagine the tabloid headlines in the *Grecian Sun* – '70-year-old philosopher condemned to death for corrupting the young'. So what was the crime of this man who was more obsessed with righteous living than any other great philosopher (Gottlieb, 2000)?

In essence, he was doing no more than challenging the powerful and trying to get the young to think for themselves. At his trial Socrates refused to waver from the beliefs that would cost him his life: 'Men of Athens, I honour and love you; but I shall obey God rather than you, and while I have life and strength I shall never cease from the practice and teaching of philosophy.'

Nevertheless, according to Athenian law, Socrates was a criminal and his condemnation was no more than just. Importantly, the French sociologist Durkheim (1858–1917), used this example to argue that crime itself can play a useful part in evolution. Crime may prepare the way for necessary changes. Socrates' crime, namely the independence of his thought, rendered a service not only to humanity but also to his country, which he loved.

Durkheim went as far as to suggest that crime is a factor in public health, an integral part of all healthy societies, stressing that a society exempt from crime is utterly impossible. Durkheim's point is that deviation is implicit in social and moral organization. It means that when specific deviations – or crimes – are brought under control and reduced or obliterated, the category of deviation nonetheless survives. In a society of saints, there will still be deviance even if it is simply the flickering of eyelids at prayers that is harshly condemned. In other words, in Durkheim's view there always will be crime and deviance, but in the so-called raising of standards it is important to recognize that the range of activity that is tolerated becomes more and more restricted. This is the problem of rigidified, totalitarian countries where the crime level is often very low.

Durkheim, however, was also concerned when the crime level in a country was, in his view, too high. With a high crime level there is the danger of anarchy and total disorder, while a low crime level could be symptomatic of an over-controlled and intolerant society. Of course, Durkheim could never reveal in concrete terms what is a reasonable crime level – or 'normal crime' in his terms. In contrast, for Karl Marx a 'healthy society' would be one free of class conflict and therefore in his terms free of crime. Hence, one can see that the functional model (or the Durkheimian approach) and the dialectic approach (or the Marxist approach) differ rather sharply on the issue of what is contributed by crime to 'all healthy societies'. Durkheim's analysis provides a warning against getting too excited about trying to eliminate crime, while the Marxist approach raises the important notion of 'power'.

Policing the powerful

It is said that the Marxist approach fell out of favour with the fall of the Berlin Wall in 1989. In truth, its demise had begun much earlier. In Britain there was much interest in Marxism in the late 1960s and early 1970s, but many criminologists recognized that their voices were not being heard in the corridors of power. The appearance of New Left Realists in the 1980s was one example of how a major theorist, Jock Young, reframed many of his ideas and began to be taken more seriously within mainstream criminology (see Young,

1986, 1992; see also chapter 5). However, in shifting too quickly from a Marxist stance (especially a conflict standpoint), there is a danger of losing important and interesting questions.

Many of the questions raised about policing make the police seem like referees on a football pitch trying to control the antics of two opposing teams. Are the police being fair, treating everyone alike – are they neutral arbiters? Conflict theorists would tend to see the police on the side of the powerful and to see the struggle as unequal. Marxists, furthermore, may highlight the dangers of likening policing to a game of football in a park and suggest that the more important questions relate to who owns the park. Analogies can be stretched too far, but there are crucial questions that should be raised as to who polices the powerful. To make some inroads into this, we will consider 'white-collar crime'.

White-collar crime

No crime blurs the boundaries more than the notion of 'white-collar crime'. It is also difficult to define. In his authoritative chapter on 'White-collar crime' in *The Oxford Handbook of Criminology* (1997), David Nelken points to 'seven types of ambiguity'. Yet much of the interest in 'white-collar crime' can be summarized as questioning whether these sorts of activities can be considered as 'crime' at all. Edwin Sutherland introduced the idea of white-collar crime to criminologists. He was not popular in doing so and many have tried to dismiss his work.

In contrast, Hermann Mannheim, a great enthusiast of the work of Sutherland, proclaimed in the second volume of his textbook *Comparative Criminology* (1965): 'there is no Nobel prize as yet for criminologists, and probably there never will be one, but if it had been available, Sutherland would have been one of the most deserving candidates for his work on WCC' (p. 470). Nelken, with somewhat less enthusiasm, says that 'if Sutherland merited a Nobel prize, as Mannheim thought . . . he certainly did not deserve it for the clarity or serviceableness of his definition' (1997: 896). In fact, Sutherland defined white-collar crime as a crime committed by 'a person of high status in the course of his occupation' (1961: 9). As Nelken stresses, the basic problem with this definition is that 'it does not distinguish crimes committed *for* an organization or business from those carried out *at its expense*' (Nelken, 1994: 361).

What has excited all the controversy? First, the sorts of activities committed *for* an organization or business, usually to increase profits – such as price fixing, the marketing of unsafe pharmaceuticals, flouting health and safety rules – rarely attract the attention of the criminal law and are even less likely to attract a prison sentence. Second, and by contrast, the activities committed *at the expense* of an organization or business – such as embezzlement or fiddling at work – are much more likely to be regarded as crime like any other crime.

To understand the controversy more fully, we need to recognize that Sutherland came to the fore in the 1930s when two criminological features were evident. First, it seemed to be a criminological truth that crime is essentially a lower-class phenomenon, so someone coming along and pointing to *white-collar* crime began to muddy the waters. Second, the 1930s were characterized by the increasing dominance of psychological explanations of criminal activity; a developing interest in psychoanalysis was given a massive boost by the escape of Jewish intellectuals, such as Sigmund Freud, from the atrocities of the Nazis in Europe prior to the Second World War. As they published more widely in English, their views became more influential. In a famous challenge to this approach, Sutherland – concerned about the wrongdoings of some major American corporations – suggested that:

> Business leaders are capable, emotionally balanced, and in no sense pathological. We have no reason to think that General Motors has an inferiority complex or that the Aluminium Company of America has a frustration–aggression complex or that U.S. Steel has an Oedipus complex, or that the Armour Company has a death wish or that Du Ponts desire to return to the womb. The assumption that an offender must have some such pathological distortion of the intellect or the emotions seems to me absurd, and if it is absurd regarding the crimes of businessmen, it is equally absurd regarding the crimes of persons in the lower economic class. (Sutherland, 1948; quoted in Mannheim, 1965)

We have little or no evidence one way or the other whether business leaders are, indeed, 'emotionally balanced'. However, the point remains that the main burden for explaining white-collar crime seems unlikely to fall upon psychological approaches, partly because the problems are widespread and so cannot be explained as aberrations.

As well as challenging class-based and psychological explanations of crime, Sutherland stirred controversy around the legal and the sociological definitions of crime. He had considered matters going through the courts relating to seventy large corporations in the United States of America. In cases where corporations had violated laws, for example, in relation to misrepresentation of advertising and infringement of patents, trademarks and copyrights, Sutherland found that only 16 per cent of decisions made against corporations were made by criminal courts. All other decisions were made by non-criminal agencies.

Paul W. Tappan became the principal spokesman of the legalistic view, arguing 'only those are criminals who have been adjudicated as such by the courts' (1947: 100). In other words, if a businessman – in order to make more profits – avoided introducing health and safety measures and this eventually led to effluent waters poisoning members of the local community, then with this approach he could be regarded as 'criminal' only if there was a criminal law against this type of behaviour – despite the amount of social harm his actions had caused. The point is that this legalistic view seems to be a very limited notion of criminal behaviour. Nevertheless, some caution is required, for there are dangers if people can be called 'criminal' just because they are doing things that we may not like.

However, a different light on the matter begins to emerge if one takes the view that much of the law protects powerful interests rather than helping vulnerable groups. It would certainly be in the interests of business corporations to avoid the rigours and penalties of the criminal law if they possibly can. Hence, the controversial issue is whether white-collar crime is still perceived as a crime (which has or can cause harm), whatever the formal, public definitions, even when it is dealt with by non-criminal processes and agencies?

Denial as a crime

Examining white-collar crime has taken us further in questioning the boundaries between crime and harm, and how, as a society, we respond to the actions of the powerful. But that debate is founded on actual misdeeds that have occurred. The discussion of 'denial' takes us into an arena in which crime can occur by omission rather than commission.

In a recent groundbreaking study that is as thought-provoking as it is disturbing, Stan Cohen (2001) explores the various states of denial that exist in modern society. Turning a blind eye and burying your head in the sand are two expressions of denial frequently used at an individual and a societal level. In high streets up and down the country, busy individuals scurry quickly past *Big Issue* sellers, so preoccupied with their own lives that they rarely stop to think about the situation of the homeless. Meanwhile, with worrying regularity, we are saturated with media images of atrocities and suffering from all over the world. Like the plight of the homeless, these images have also become normalized. They are commonplace. So, too, Cohen suggests, is our apparent indifference.

Moving from the personal to the political, Cohen examines how organized atrocities, such as the Holocaust and other genocides, are denied by perpetrators and by bystanders. Bystander nations are those who do nothing, frequently claiming in the aftermath of an event that they were unaware of what was taking place. As for perpetrators, one of the strategies that they use is what Cohen describes as 'interpretive denial', claiming that what is happening is really something else. This is particularly evident in the euphemistic language used by organizations devoted to committing atrocities. The Nazi 'euthanasia' programme for killing the mentally handicapped and other supposedly unworthy people was renamed the Charitable Foundation for Institutional Care. This deliberate misrepresentation is not unique. In the 1970s Idi Amin's death squads in Uganda were officially known as the State Research Bureau (Cohen, 2001: 107).

Denial of past atrocities, such as the Holocaust in the Second World War, is now regarded as a crime in several countries. It is hoped that acknowledgement of genocide in the past may prevent the likelihood of further abuses in the future. Denial laws derive from the more general use of the criminal law against 'hate' crimes, crimes committed for racial or religious reasons.

Many regard the Holocaust as a historical event firmly embedded in our past, something that could not possibly happen again. Yet genocide continues; less than ten years ago it happened again, this time in central Africa where hundreds of thousands of Rwandans were slaughtered as the world watched. In 1994 more than half a million people, three-quarters of the Tutsi minority in Rwanda, were slaughtered within 100 days. This was the swiftest genocide of the twentieth century, and in the years since this atrocity it has generally been accepted that several major international players knew about the impending slaughter and did nothing to prevent it. They were what Cohen would most probably describe as 'bystander nations'.

A report by the organization Human Rights Watch was published in May 1999 and entitled 'Leave none to tell the story: genocide in Rwanda'. Based on evidence from government records, the report criticizes the UN, the USA, France and Belgium for knowing about preparations for the killings and not taking any action. In May 1994 the then UN secretary-general, Boutros-Ghali, admitted that the international community had failed the people of Rwanda in not putting a stop to the genocide. Since then, the former US president, Bill Clinton, has apologized for not having responded to Rwandan cries for help. The subsequent secretary-general of the United Nations, Kofi Anan, has expressed regret in vaguer terms and various world leaders have acknowledged responsibility for their failure to intervene.

Yet according to the Human Rights Watch:

> Much of the truth remains hidden, however, by the laws, regulations and practices long used to protect political leaders from accountability . . . Researchers must continue trying to go beyond the relatively painless, generalised confessions of political leaders to analyse decisions taken by individuals, so that these persons can be obliged to acknowledge their responsibilities at least in the public domain, if not in a court of law. Only in this way can we hope to influence decision makers in the future to never again abandon a people to genocidal slaughter. (Human Rights Watch, 1999)

The notion, then, of culpable nations whose criminality lies in omission as well as commission extends both the definitions of the offender as well as those of the crime itself. Crime retains its defining element of power over others, but in this case it is the *refusal* to exercise superior physical power.

There is much else that is unpleasant and questionable in the exercise of power beyond genocide alone. Mary Daly (1979), a radical feminist, points to the male domination of women, or *patriarchy*, which she suggests is everywhere expressed through the systematic destruction or mutilation of women. Different cultures express this in different ways: suttee (the burning alive of widows) in India; foot-binding in China; female circumcision in Muslim Africa; the burning of witches in Europe; and gynaecological therapies such as hysterectomy in modern America ('*gynocide*', as Daly terms it). Should there be international intervention to stop such practices that reflect the male domination of women?

Our judgements of the powerful and their potential abuses of power change over time. It is reported, for example, that the Home Office has backed an investigation by Wiltshire police into the behaviour of Porton Down scientists in the 1950s and 1960s. Porton Down was home to official investigations into chemical warfare, and thousands of soldiers volunteered to act as human guinea pigs. But now it is reported that they were, at the time, duped into taking part, believing experiments to be concerned with finding a cure for the common cold (*Independent on Sunday*, 26 August 2001, p. 11). Are the scientists' actions judged to have been criminal at the time of commission, or is it according to current values that, retrospectively, we reassess such harmful actions?

The policing of protest

Concern at official exercise of power can lead to protest; hence it may arise when representative democracy seems to fail. Thus protest is often interpreted as a challenge to the legitimacy of government rather than as a social order issue. A basic problem for the authorities, then, is that they often do not know how to handle protest. Attempts are made to marginalize protesters, and their activities are vulnerable to becoming criminalized. As criminologists, we need to recognize that there are different kinds of protest which represent different sorts of challenge to accepted ways of doing things.

Traditionally, criminologists have made the distinction between aberrant behaviour and non-conforming behaviour. In fact, aberrant and non-conforming behaviours are alike in that they move away from identifiable social norms. However, the 'aberrant' simply violates the rules and tries to get away with it – without denouncing those rules or proposing alternatives. In contrast, the 'non-conformist' announces dissent publicly, challenging the legitimacy of the social norms they are rejecting and aiming to change the norms being denied. With non-conforming behaviour, conventional members, albeit reluctantly, acknowledge that rule-breaking is for disinterested purposes, while, with aberrant behaviour, the person is assumed to be deviating from norms to serve their own interests (Merton, 1966).

While such a divide has much meaning, it may be too narrow a framework for understanding the range of protest seen in the last two decades, such as the newspaper production dispute at Wapping (1986/7), the miners' strike (1984/5), the Greenham Common protest (1981) and the poll tax riots (1990). Like the protests of the French farmers, which disrupted both holidaymakers and business traffic at the Channel ports in the late 1990s, the strikes of British miners and the protests at Wapping could be seen as matters of self-interest. Yet they could also be described as attempts to conserve ways of life and working conditions for future generations. All can be interpreted as protest against *ways* of enforcing legitimate power, whether through imposition of industrial change or the storing of Cruise missiles.

Protests can range from campaigns that excite little interest or controversy to protests that seem to connect with widespread civil unrest. They may be one-issue campaigns, such as the long-lasting Campaign against Nuclear Disarmament, which first reached its height in the early 1960s; the aims of other campaigns and protests can be more diffuse. The concern of governments is often that protests about redundancies (such as the miners' strike of 1984/5) or demonstrations about taxes (such as the poll tax demonstrations of 1990) can escalate or, indeed, mask wider challenges to government. Sim and colleagues note how:

> The period from the early 1970s onwards has been dominated both by the question of Britain's economic decline and by the ongoing struggle to maintain order and cohesion on a number of fronts. The uprisings in 1981 and 1985 and the confrontations between the police and different groups and communities have demonstrated both the fragility of that order and the limitations in the repertoire of the state's response. These limitations have been illustrated clearly in the ongoing struggle to maintain order in Northern Ireland. (Sim et al., 1987: 50–1)

Certainly, the then prime minister, Margaret Thatcher, was convinced when she stated: 'I had never any doubt about the true aim of the hard Left: they were revolutionaries who sought to impose a Marxist system on Britain whatever the means and whatever the cost' ('Mr Scargill's Insurrection', Thatcher, 1993: 339). Similarly, Thatcher talks of the poll tax, which replaced the rating system with a community charge, in a chapter entitled 'A little local difficulty'. She noted how:

> On Saturday 31 March, the day before the introduction of the community charge in England and Wales, a demonstration against the charge degenerated into rioting in and around Trafalgar Square . . . Almost 400 policemen were injured and 339 people were arrested. It was a mercy that no one was killed. I was appalled at such wickedness. (1993: 661)

She further notes that 'the eventual abandonment of the charge represented one of the greatest victories for these people ever conceded by a Conservative government' (p. 661).

The boundary, then, between aberrant and non-conforming behaviour, between self-interest and a wider protest, can be blurred. It depends, in part, on one's vantage point. Take, for example, the story of Robin Hood, the heroic figure from English folklore, who (story has it) lived and behaved outside of the law. Few people probably ever consider Robin Hood's criminal record, but at the very least it would have included criminal damage, breaking and entering, robbery, burglary, violence against the person and (depending on which version of the Hollywood movie you watch) possibly also murder. Hood was regarded as a hero in folklore rather than condemned for his actions, especially as he supposedly redistributed wealth. Probably the important point is that although his methods may have been criminal – in that they were in breach of the law – his motives were not deemed immoral.

The danger for the authorities begins when an apparent consensus over what constitutes crime starts to break down and protest is a part of rapid social change. Robin Hood was certainly hated by the authorities, but his activities were a form of protest which the populace generally (and particularly the poor of Sherwood Forest) applauded. The famous historian, G. M. Trevelyan, traces the growing but disparate challenge to the dominance of the class of landowning gentry, whose power had replaced that of the great nobles and ecclesiastics of the feudal ages:

> The bands of 'sturdy beggars' who alarmed society in the early Tudor reigns were recruited from many sources – the ordinary unemployed, the unemployable, soldiers discharged after French wars and the Wars of the Roses . . . Robin Hood bands driven from their woodland lairs by deforestation and by the better enforcement of the King's peace, ploughmen put out of work by enclosures for pastures, and tramps who pretended to belong to that much commiserated class. All through the Tudor reigns, the 'beggars coming to town' preyed on the fears of dwellers in lonely farms and hamlets, and exercised the minds of magistrates, Privy Councillors, and Parliaments. (Trevelyan, 1964: 218–19)

Trevelyan's analysis underlines the Robin Hood story by reminding us that there are people whose very way of life is seen as protest, as a challenge to authority. This confusion between policing difference and policing public order was not a Tudor problem alone. More recently, the camp set up by women at Greenham Common represented an alternative lifestyle that was, of itself, a permanent reminder of protest at the presence of US weapons. From the 1970s onwards the numbers of 'new age travellers' grew in Britain – living in buses and caravans and moving from place to place. The annual free festival at Stonehenge was one focus for gatherings of new age travellers; and the 1985 gathering saw what became known as the 'battle of the beanfield'. A large-scale police operation dispersed the gathering. By all accounts, police tactics were extremely violent and, most certainly, the press demonized travellers (see Greenleaf; Tash). Rosenberger (2001) links the policing of raves with the policing of travellers (see 'Policing of pleasure', below).

We have seen with the story of the outlaw Robin Hood that criminal behaviour may be interpreted as moral when we accept the justness of the underlying cause. The wider moral purpose said to separate aberrant from non-conformist behaviour could be said to distinguish terrorist activity too. So, why is Socrates (see above) regarded as a 'criminal' and not a 'terrorist'? Why is Osama bin Laden (widely regarded as the brains behind the atrocities of 11 September 2001, the destruction of the World Trade Centre in New York) targeted as a 'terrorist' and not as a 'criminal'? Is it the scale of the harm? No, if a serial killer murdered 6,000 victims, they would still be regarded as a criminal unless they proclaimed that it was all done on behalf of some political cause.

However, the notion of a political or religious cause is not the litmus test. Both Socrates and Osama bin Laden seem to appeal to some kind of higher morality which is supposed to justify their actions. However, whereas Socrates accepted the legitimacy of his condemners – he agreed that his condemnation was just – terrorists do not accept the legitimacy of the court in which they are tried. The boundary is when legitimate protest moves into criminal activity (that is, breaking the criminal law) or terrorist activity (which is both breaking the law – national or international – and not accepting the legitimacy of the law). In this way, terrorists not only threaten public order and commit crime, but they challenge the social framework of the societies under attack.

The authorities can police protest in at least two ways. First, they can create more laws that make the scope for peaceful protest increasingly difficult. In effect, this is criminalizing aspects of protest and thus makes it more likely that a protest will be designated as criminal activity. To some degree this has happened in relation to picketing, a concept and activity that has been restricted only to the site of the dispute. Similarly, Rosenberger (2001) argues that section

39 of the Public Order Act 1986 was a response to the 'battle of the beanfield', to ensure that new age travellers were placed on the wrong side of the law. Second, the authorities can monitor the protest itself by trying to ensure that the protest keeps within the existing law. The policing choices made will depend on the extent to which the protest is seen to represent a wider social challenge beyond its immediate cause.

Protesters can be scapegoated as criminals, particularly if they are engaged in highlighting an issue that makes the government uncomfortable. However, there is also a danger in romanticizing protest, and not all those who attend protest meetings have a message to put across. Protesters tend to mask or deny the dangers of the protest. Nevertheless, the authorities demonize protestors when they exaggerate the scale of criminal activity and so contribute to a denial of the authenticity of the protest (see 'Denial as a crime', above). Interestingly, protests may also produce or reveal divisions within society, and those involved in dispensing justice may not always behave in expected ways (see box 7.1).

In fact, green activists face a lottery as to whether they are likely to be found guilty or not guilty, depending on which court they appear before. While court cases may be very different in reality from the truncated versions that appear in the media, magistrates and judges do not appear to be dispensing justice in the same way in Middlesex, Norwich, Durham, Liverpool, Chelmsford, Weymouth or Wood Green (see box 7.2).

Protest can be noisy, peaceful, violent, small-scale, disturbing of the peace and challenging to social order. With the continuing troubles in Northern Ireland, industrial disputes, anti-capitalism demonstrations and the resurgence of international terrorism, there is always the ongoing struggle to maintain order and cohesion. Protest will remain a contested issue, deemed a part of popular expression, especially where the powerful are not listening to legitimate grievance. Yet protest is capable of being both threatening and criminal.

What now remains to be confronted is another boundary that sometimes seems to be heavily policed – namely, the policing of pleasure. Why do we need to control pleasures so avidly?

Policing of pleasure

The end of the ban on D. H. Lawrence's book, *Lady Chatterley's Lover* – considered as 'the seminal text for comprehending the

---

BOX 7.1   MAGISTRATES ACQUIT GM CROP PROTESTERS

Seven protesters who dressed as grim reapers and cut down and trampled on a genetically modified maize crop in a protest over government trials were acquitted yesterday by Weymouth magistrates of aggravated trespass.

It is thought to be the first time that magistrates rather than a jury have acquitted GM protesters. Since the Greenpeace trial when Lord Melchett and others were acquitted, there has been official concern that juries are more likely to take the protesters' side.

On hearing the news, several local people visited another GM field near Weymouth and started to pull the crop down. No one was arrested.

The GM maize was about 5 ft high when the seven defendants and about ninety others invaded a 33 acre field at Tolbridge Farm near Sherborne, Dorset, on 16 July last year.

Magistrates were shown a police video of protesters in the field. About a third of the crop was damaged in the non-violent protest. The court was told that the seven defendants had told police during interviews that they were in the field, and said they were protesting about the use of genetically modified maize, which they considered dangerous.

Aventis product development manager Judith Jordan told the court that the GM crop was part of a trial to test its herbicide resistance.

The case collapsed after arguments that the charge of aggravated trespass did not stand up.

Source: *Guardian*, 13 June 2001

---

mystical rapture of mutual simultaneous orgasm as a holy rite' (Haste, 1992: 76) – was a major watershed in the challenge to the policing of pleasure, but only one milestone.

This case was the first challenge to the Obscene Publications Act 1959, which aimed to protect literature but strengthen the law against pornography (Haste, 1992: 177). The director of public prosecutions decided in 1960 to prosecute Penguin Books for publishing Lawrence's book in a 3s. 6d. paperback edition. The prosecuting counsel,

BOX 7.2   STALKING THE BOUNDARIES

The trials and tribulations of green activists

Not guilty   June 2001, Wood Green Crown Court. Frank Guterbock and Janet Miller and three other Greenpeace volunteers are found not guilty of criminal damage after occupying Edmonton incinerator.

Not guilty   June 2001, Weymouth magistrates. Rowan Tilly, Chris Black, David Cooper and four others found not guilty of aggravated trespass when they pulled up GM maize in Dorset.

Guilty   May 2001, Chelmsford Crown Court. Susan Van der Hijden and Martin Newall jailed for one year for burglary with intent and criminal damage to a Trident nuclear convoy at RAF Wittering.

Not guilty   January 2001, Liverpool Crown Court. Sylvia Boyes and Keith Wright found not guilty by majority verdict of conspiracy to commit criminal damage to HMS *Vengeance*.

Guilty   December 2000. Five people found guilty of pulling up GM crop in Co. Durham. The defendants are given conditional discharges and not ordered to pay costs.

Not guilty   September 2000, Norwich Crown Court. Lord Melchett and 27 Greenpeace volunteers are acquitted of criminal damage after destroying part of a GM maize field in Norfolk.

Guilty   December 1999, Middlesex Crown Court. Helen John found guilty of criminal damage to the Houses of Parliament. She had written on it 'ban Trident'. The jury stated that they 'unanimously agreed that the defendant had a reasonable cause for her action'. Sentencing was deferred until last month when she was jailed for three months.

Not guilty   November 1999, Tommy Archer, of Radio 4's *The Archers*, acquitted by a fictional jury of destroying a GM crop.

Not guilty   October 1999, Greenock Sheriff Court. Angie Zelter, Ellen Moxley and Ulla Roder cleared of criminal damage to a Trident research barge.

Source: *Guardian*, 28 June 2001

Mervyn Griffith Jones, showed that the trial really concerned the *widespread* reading about sex when he invited the jury to ask themselves if it was 'a book that you would have lying around in your own house? Is it a book that you would even wish your wife or your servants to read?' (1992: 178). In other words, the male ruling elite could enjoy such pleasures, but should it be extended to others? The publishers were acquitted. The case was seen as a major and successful challenge to the state's right to control individual morality.

There was considerable overlap between law and morality as shown in figure 7.1(a). Historically, an absolute morality has been imposed on the populace by the ruling elite, using the law as one of the strong mechanisms to effect this. In a lecture to the British Academy on 'The enforcement of morals', published in 1959, Lord Devlin maintained that every society had the right to pass judgement on matters of morals and to enforce its judgement by force of law (Mannheim, 1965, vol. 1: 54). He was perhaps the last eminent judge to put such a view so forcefully, and the statement was made on the threshold of significant change. However, gradually, the law and morality separated much more, as figure 7.1(b) indicates. This produces three categories of behaviour:

1   illegal behaviour sanctioned by law, but which is not commonly considered anti-social (Morris, 1958);
2   anti-social action which is illegal, and is sanctioned by both law and public opinion;
3   anti-social action which is not illegal, and is sanctioned only by public opinion.

It would be misleading to think that public opinion is necessarily quite so clear-cut. In figure 7.1(c) we have tried to illustrate the increasingly fragmented and diverse range of 'public opinions', for nowadays there are many audiences to address and to listen to. In other words, there are many different kinds of moral codes to which people adhere.

Sexual reforms – such as allowing abortion and the practice of homosexuality – reached the political agenda in the 1960s as issues of social justice and personal liberty. Haste, commenting on this era, notes that: 'Young people were seen as the catalysts of change in the search for a new morality because conventional values of sexual restraint no longer commanded their allegiance. They were to remain

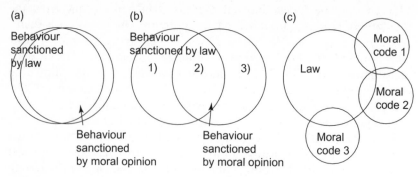

Figure 7.1   The relationship between the law and morality

the agents of change during the next decade' (1992: 184). So what actually was happening?

Increasingly, there was concern at the use of the criminal law to impose a particular brand of morality on the community when there was no evidence of causing real harm. The blurring of these boundaries started with the Chatterley case. The title of a song – 'Sex and drugs and rock and roll' – by the late British rock singer, Ian Dury, ably summarizes the contested terrain of the last forty years. The battleground sometimes seems like the policing of pleasure, and especially the pleasures liked by the young rather than the old.

The list is a long one and includes the age of consent for various sexual activities, licensing hours, raves, pornography, soft drugs, hard drugs and film censorship. It is impossible to draw the threads of all the debates on these issues together, but many relate to what has been described as the emergence of the 'leisure problem' (Clarke and Critcher, 1985: 12). Mostly, they reflect concerns about how youth should spend its leisure time and how stringently it should be policed. However, the 'leisure problem' has, historically, been concerned with what the working classes should be allowed to do when they are not working.

Leisure is an important ingredient in a capitalist society in which the 'Protestant work ethic' has been the paramount value over the past 300 years. However, while work, for most people, is identified as drudgery, containing little *intrinsic* satisfaction and largely undertaken for the money that allows needs to be satisfied outside work, 'leisure seems to offer the prospect of being all those things that work is not: the source of satisfactions, gratifications and pleasures' (Clarke and Critcher, 1985: 3). These authors go on to indicate that the boundaries of leisure and crime seem to overlap and quickly become blurred: 'Free time seems to be inconveniently associated with the 'devil's work' rather than emancipation: drunkenness, illicit sexuality, crime, violence, vandalism, physical and psychological demoralisation and urban riots' (1985: 4). Lord Scarman writing on the causes of the Brixton riots of 1981 suggested the interconnections of free time and undesirable consequences:

> It is clear that the exuberance of youth requires in Brixton (and other similar inner city areas) imaginative and socially acceptable opportunities for release if it is not to become frustrated or to be diverted to criminal ends. It is equally clear that such opportunities do not at present exist for young people in Brixton to the extent that they ought, particularly given the enforced idleness of many youths through unemployment. The amusement arcades, the unlawful drinking clubs, and, I believe, the criminal classes gain as a result. (Scarman, 1981: 6–7)

Here the concern is about the lack of 'suitable' opportunities for release and the dangers arising from what is available. From the viewpoint of the participants, leisure is emancipation, away from the constraints of work. For those in positions of power – the employers and anyone else who wants to control the populace – leisure is the 'dark entanglement of idleness and vice' (Clarke and Critcher, 1985: 5). Clarke and Critcher go on to suggest that, to complement the Protestant work ethic, there is also a Protestant *leisure* ethic: 'free time – to avoid the descent into the murky waters of idleness and the devil's work – has to be "constructive". It has to be spent wisely' (1985: 5). The interest is in leisure being carefully controlled owing to the fear of freedom and its *illicit* pleasures.

Historically, the authorities' concern about pleasure has been that it may intrude into work patterns. Kohn (1992: 29) has described how laws passed in times of emergency remain long after the crisis has passed. So, the Defence of the Realm Act (DORA) was passed after the outbreak of the First World War (1914) to control communication of sensitive information. For the sake of wartime production, however, DORA also restricted pub licensing hours and drinking. Kohn argues that DORA stretched further to include control of drug-taking, during a wave of anti-drug panic in the first decades of the twentieth century: in 1916 regulation 40B of DORA made illegal the possession of cocaine and opium, apart from by professionals such as doctors or chemists (1992: 43–4).

Another major concern has been that pleasures may lead to a lack of control, and the dangers of disorder are always a paramount concern. Rosenberger (2001) comments that public responses in 1992 to the crowds of young people travelling round the countryside looking for the sites of rave parties got caught up with a newspaper outcry about new age travellers: 'The tabloid press in particular were scandalised by the apparent ability of these two groups to set up events of 20,000 people despite police efforts to prevent them' (2001: 4). Rosenberger argues that this led to tough anti-protest sections in the Criminal Justice and Public Order Act 1994, with increased police powers to prevent public assemblies.

Much of the policing of pleasure, of course, is justified on the basis that some pleasures may harm. This claim does have a reality to it, but rarely to the extent that is often suggested. An interesting contribution to the debate has been offered by Parker et al. in their book *Illegal Leisure* (1998). According to the authors, recreational drug use 'is both about risk taking but also about taking "time out" to self-medicate the impact of the stresses and strains of both successes and failures in "modern" times' (1998: 152). With the development of the 'health' police, trying to stop people doing things that may damage their health will become an increasingly contentious issue in the twenty-first century. In what ways should the criminal law be involved in policing such activities for this reason? Libertarians may challenge such an intrusion and suggest that the activities of the 'health' police may mask a moral crusade as well. In other words, perhaps some of the concerns are about what we find *morally* acceptable rather than simply a focus on health. But even if it is simply the latter, should the criminal law really be used to stop people killing themselves? The debate is not an easy one.

The policing of pleasures now has global repercussions. Mark Bowden's book *Killing Pablo* (2001) focuses on Pablo Emilio Escobar Gaviria (1949–93), considered by some as the most talented of the Colombian drug bosses. The sub-title – *The Hunt for the Richest, Most Powerful Criminal in History* – gives a clue to some of the stakes involved. However, the situation is volatile:

Until 11 September [the date of the attack on the twin towers of the World Trade Centre and the Pentagon], every arm of the security bureaucracy – the CIA, the FBI, the Armed Forces and the Coast Guard – were involved to a greater or lesser extent, under the hapless overall control of the DEA [Drug Enforcement Agency], in the war of drugs, which mostly took a higher priority than the prevention of terrorism. But things are changing dramatically and the sudden redeployment of resources is consistent with the growing view that decriminalising drugs and abandoning a war on that front are the most sensible ways forward. (Luttwak, 2001)

This has echoes of the original Prohibition – of alcohol in the USA (1920–33) – which was seen as a political compromise, bringing together issues of moral welfare, concern for workers' lives and health and social upheaval in the face of immigration. An outcome of sophisticated political lobbying, Prohibition is commonly thought to have triggered a crime wave of bootlegging, illicit manufacturing of alcohol, speakeasies and corruption in public life. Support for Prohibition faded, too, in the face of pressing political concerns, most notably the depression of the 1930s (see Behr, 1997).

Whether considering the crimes of the powerful, the politics of protest or the policing of pleasures, global issues increasingly obtrude. The boundaries that define crime are, perhaps, not always so obvious as we would like to imagine. Global concerns make the defining of crime even more complex, but the interrelationships that emerge produce another problem: what are the boundaries of criminology in this increasingly complex world? This is the final issue to which we now turn.

8

Criminology in a Changing World

This final chapter questions what constitutes criminology, and highlights
the dangers of defining it too narrowly. We consider some of the challenges
ahead for the criminology of the future, especially the need to respond to
wider global changes. Finally, we ask if there are dangers in using the
criminal law as the main means of social control.

In this chapter we consider some of the challenges that criminology
has to face in a changing world. We need to assess where criminology is and what our hopes and fears for its future are. This means
examining how criminology's boundaries are being defined and,
indeed, examining the dangers of over-definition. Criminology faces
new challenges – especially the impact of globalization. We conclude
by looking at the future of the issue which, for many people, underpins the whole enterprise of studying crime – that of 'crime control' –
and ask what dangers lie in using the criminal law as our main form
of social control.

There are increasing attempts to make criminology academically
respectable, and increasing numbers of undergraduates in Britain are
studying criminology. There may be different names for the courses
(for example, criminal justice studies, critical criminology, or crime,
deviance and society) but behind all these initiatives is the study of
criminology.

Respectability can bring blandness. As the American poet and playwright Imamu Amiri Baraka has suggested in another context, 'God

has been replaced, as he has all over the West, with respectability and air-conditioning'. The Irish playwright George Bernard Shaw claimed: 'The more things a man is ashamed of, the more respectable he is.'

Has criminology a past, or even a present, to be ashamed of? Criminology is essentially a bastard discipline, not really sure of its parentage – different interests within criminology claim different parentage. There are both technical and moral aspects to the discipline. Certainly, if the underlying science is wrong – as it was with the early Lombrosian approach – then the applications can be disastrous. There can be even more problems if the underlying science seems to be right, for this puts the pressure on deciding the appropriate application.

For example, what policy implications are there if it is shown that black people commit more crime than white people? Theoretically, one could go down the eugenics route and try to eliminate this part of the population. Alternatively, one could go down the more sociological route of trying to overcome the structural inequalities that beset some groups in society. The important point here is that criminologists cannot both claim their importance and dissociate from how criminological findings might be used. They have a moral obligation to consider the practical implications of their work.

For there are important threats on the horizon. In particular, the claims of some geneticists are a potential threat to the whole discipline of criminology, as there is little point to a study of activities that are predestined from birth or before.

New developments in the area of genetics could certainly pose problems for the criminal law (see box 8.1). Equally, however, genetics may provide new insights that need to be properly evaluated and drawn into the body of knowledge we describe as criminology.

Elizabeth Barrett Browning asked of respectability, 'when was genius found respectable'? Mr Pickwick in Charles Dickens' *Pickwick Papers* talked of the 'eccentricities of genius'. So, is a concern with academic respectability in criminology likely to limit insightful and original work? In our view, answers to these concerns rest on how criminology's boundaries become defined and how they are, in the future, policed.

Defining criminology's boundaries

There are many good reasons to define the limits and boundaries of criminology. An increasing desire among some criminologists is to

BOX 8.1   THE CRIMINAL GENE

With the new genetics, it is becoming easier to blame all bad conduct on DNA. Acts once thought of as the result of poor upbringing are more and more ascribed to inborn weakness.

Badly behaved children were once seen as free spirits, to be controlled when necessary. Now though, there is a disease known as attention deficit hyperactivity disorder, ADHD. Its symptoms include poor concentration and a general tendency to run riot. In the USA it is epidemic. In some classrooms, a quarter of pupils are diagnosed as having it.

Why is the disease (if such it is) so common? Blame has been directed at everything from soft drinks to computer games. Some psychiatrists, though, think that genes are involved. A difficult child is much more likely to get into trouble when adult. In Britain, a quarter of all crimes are carried out by a hard core of 3 per cent of all young offenders. Many continue their criminal careers as adults.

Childish bad behaviour and adult crime, then, spring from the same source: that is, at least in part, genetic. Some enthusiasts suggest that half the prison population is there because their genes predispose them to ADHD. If this is true, prisons are as much institutions for the genetically unlucky as places of punishment.

Imagine the problem that will emerge as genetic arguments are used in court. If a child's outrageous conduct in school is excused because of an inherited flaw, it is hard not to permit the same excuse in adulthood. When, as in the USA, more children are diagnosed with ADHD than there are adult criminals, then many of those who offend may soon be able to appeal to genes in mitigation.

The law cannot, it is clear, accept this. Although it may be obliged to admit that for many people free will is constrained by genes, their actions must be treated as intentional, because good order demands it. Even if most of those who offend do so because of an inborn weakness, the law must ignore the fact.

Society is not a product of genes but of people, and what they do must be judged by the law and not by science. There can be no universal defence for bad behaviour. If some are excused because of their biology, then others become relatively more culpable. Predisposition is a double-edged sword. If most criminals offend because of the genes they carry, the scope for mitigation becomes so wide as to lose its meaning. For the law to survive, it must ignore the defence of inherited frailty, in much the same way as it ignores poverty, inborn or not.

Source: Adapted from 'The criminal gene' by Professor Steve Jones, *Daily Telegraph*, 27 April 1996

identify the core issues, perhaps the core values, of criminology. People studying criminology do need to know what the subject purports to be; and they do need to know about crime, about the justice system, about justice, about theory and about policy. Most academic subjects of study are going through a process of benchmarking that involves, in part, identifying the key skills expected of graduates.

Hence, charting the boundaries of a discipline may have two broad purposes: first, delineating the boundaries of an academic area so that everyone will know (within certain limits) what skills and insights graduates in particular subjects have achieved; second, clarifying the boundaries so that someone can *practise* a subject. The former is appropriate for an academic subject, while the latter is appropriate for a *practical* subject in the sense that the person wishes to *practise*. Clarifying the boundaries is much more important when the second purpose is in the frame. Few would like to be operated on for a stomach complaint by a doctor who has not acquired the appropriate skills. Yet, as we have seen in chapter 6, criminology *is* an applied subject, albeit in contested and complex ways.

In contrast, there are learned societies that disseminate knowledge and communicate innovations, through conferences and through publishing journals. Currently, the main learned society for criminologists in Britain is the British Society of Criminology (BSC). There has been no attempt to restrict the title of 'criminologist', and anyone, both within and without the BSC, can use the term.

We started this book by describing criminology as a discourse, that is, a debate about ways of assessing and evaluating information to do with crime and about ways of knowing about crime and criminals. While, as we have seen, there are good reasons for delineating the boundaries of criminology as a subject of study at university, there are dangers for the richness of the discourse in how this is done. Below we consider two major, interrelated, dangers:

- narrowness
- policing the boundaries too rigorously

Narrowness

The first danger is that criminology will be defined too narrowly. In the past, some have tried to claim that it should be limited to behaviour proscribed by the criminal law but, as we saw in chapter 7, Sutherland's work on white-collar crime began to challenge that conception. The desire to define criminology narrowly follows from an attempt to identify academic territory that is not already occupied by other disciplines. With its focus specifically on crime, criminology, in turn, has a different perspective to offer. However, its strength is that it embraces and feeds off other disciplines, especially sociology and psychology. Hence, claiming exclusivity of knowledge is a dangerous path to follow. Indeed, Garland and Sparks argue that 'defending the disciplinary identity of criminology against incursions from "elsewhere" is now as unfeasible as it is undesirable . . . the conception of criminology as an autonomous and self-standing discipline is one that belongs to an earlier stage of its historical development' (2000: 2–3).

A problem allied with defining criminology too narrowly is the growing pattern that criminology students study only criminology. To use Matza's term, one needs to be much more appreciative of other disciplines (1969) and this means studying these other disciplines seriously. To take one example: the old study of 'social administration' (now largely replaced by 'social policy' and 'applied social science'), probed the historical development of the British welfare state and studied the current complexities met by – for instance – claimants on benefits. Many, if not most, offenders have been claimants at some point in their lives; hence a failure on the part of criminologists to understand the workings and the shortcomings of the British welfare state is a deficiency.

Thirty years ago, people writing about criminological topics necessarily came into criminology from other academic areas because specialized courses were few. They often had a rich pedigree of other work – in politics, psychology, sociology, economics or medicine –

but their grounding in basic criminology could often be thin. Nowadays, the opposite is likely to be the case. The grounding in the basic criminological topics is becoming increasingly rich, but the recognition that other disciplines impinge on criminology is being lost.

We saw in chapter 6 that there is a danger of seeing criminology *either* as social commentary *or* as a technical subject. With the intellectual challenge to and the demise of 'the Lombrosian project' and the increasing ascendancy of what Garland has called 'the governmental project', particular questions are returning to the fore. We noted in chapter 6 that all sponsors of research – the Home Office, the ESRC (which receives much of its funding from the government) or charitable organizations – fund research that reflects their own interests and agendas. This is rightly so, for why would they fund research that is not of immediate relevance to their enterprises?

There is, however, a danger of returning to the debates of the 1960s and 1970s, when radical criminologists had legitimate concerns about being tainted by state-sponsored research (albeit holding on to university posts funded by the state). More recent concerns have been raised about the narrowness of, for instance, evaluation studies (see Morgan, 2000, quoted in chapter 6) and the difficulties for researchers to produce *questioning* analyses when carrying out funded research. Previously, there was much concern in the academic community over whether governments would censor research containing uncomfortable findings for the government. Uncomfortable findings can take a long time to gain approval, with the result that a politically difficult moment can be allowed to pass.

These concerns need to be tackled if criminology is to succeed as an applied study. Both approaches have their place, and a strong learned society can support funded researchers in negotiating the realities of producing questioning research in the 'administrative sphere'. Likewise, social commentators in criminology need to acknowledge that government research, especially, has moved on since the 1970s (a brief glance at the Home Office research and publishing website shows an astonishing range of activities). Rather than returning to the solutions of criminology's grandparents, there is room to recognize that the framework within which this debate takes place between sponsors of research and criminologists (and between different criminologists) can be more dynamic and interactive than might, previously, have been the case.

While individual researchers may specialize, there is a danger in mistaking these personal choices for the whole of what criminology should be. We have commented earlier that the implications of criminological research and theory may well have an impact on the lives of real people. Therefore, criminologists have a moral obligation to consider the potential impact of their work *and* an obligation to ensure that their research is as skilled and professional as it can be.

Policing the boundaries

The second major concern is the danger of policing the boundaries of criminology too rigorously. We want the booklists of criminology students to range widely. So, for example, Tony Parker, who has been the most outstanding interviewer of criminals since the Second World War, must not be forgotten following his death. Described as the 'Mayhew of his times', his work spanned the 1960s and 1990s and he speaks intimately to all kinds of offenders – inadequates, professional criminals, sex offenders, fraudsters and false pretences merchants. His work is both timely and timeless and is recaptured in an anthology, *Criminal Conversations* (Soothill, 1999). Yet would he be accepted as a criminologist today? He had no training in criminology; indeed he never went to university.

Other writers, also from outside academe, have offered insights into some of society's most troubling and difficult issues. Blake Morrison's *As If* (1997) is a haunting account arising out of the murder of Liverpool toddler James Bulger but focusing on the children who murdered him and their trial. It is a compassionate yet clear-sighted account of, and response to, an event that society has found hard to contemplate – that of children murdering children. Similarly, Gitta Sereny has written of such unpopular characters as Nazi war criminal Albert Speer and has also addressed the phenomenon of children who murder children. There was a public outcry when she updated her account of child-murderer Mary Bell with an account – based on interviews with the adult Mary – of her life (see Sereny, 1998). Morrison and Sereny are each more easily described as a distinguished writer and journalist.

There are others from within the academic world – such as Marie Tatar, Professor of German at Harvard University – who would almost certainly not wish to be called a criminologist. However, her book *Lustmord: Sexual Murder in Weimar Germany* is a riveting study of how art and murder have intersected in the sexual politics of culture from Weimar Germany to the present. It perhaps begins to help to explain why Germany is known to have had a series of serial killers between the two world wars, while England seems to have had none. In brief, much is relevant to criminology, and some of the more intellectually inspirational works are not being written by criminologists.

The aim of highlighting these dangers is not to question the existence of criminology but to widen its horizons. It is inevitable that criminology will change over time. Indeed, there has been a rapid expansion of criminology courses in the university sector in recent years. However, we argue that changes should encompass a broad perspective on crime, particularly when criminology is facing fresh challenges as a consequence of massive changes in the wider society.

Globalization

Globalization refers to the increasing interdependence and inter-connectedness of the modern world. For some critics globalization has eroded distinct cultural identities, with the streets of major cities all over the world increasingly resembling each other, dominated as they are by the same 'global' enterprises such as McDonalds, Sony and Coca-Cola. Others argue that globalization is a consequence of capitalism, which has served only to increase the unequal distribution of wealth between rich and poor countries. In recent times, international organizations such as the World Trade Organisation and the International Monetary Fund have come under persistent attack from anti-capitalist protesters who are critical of the immense amount of financial power that these organizations wield.

Yet other commentators point to the advantages of globalization, noting that we should make the most of the new opportunities available to us. For example, the advance of telecommunications, in particular the Internet, has enabled split-second communication with people all over the world. Global enthusiasts argue that the growth of trade between nations can increase the wealth of everyone. International co-operation can strengthen relationships between different countries, enabling them to learn from each other.

But what does all this mean for criminology? Regardless of whether we view globalization as a good or a bad phenomenon, the simple fact is that the world is changing, and as it evolves, criminology also needs to evolve. No longer can our interests be narrowly national. What is happening in one part of the world can much more directly affect another part of the world. Indeed in a speech to the Economic

Club of Chicago, USA, in April 1999, British Prime Minister Tony Blair noted that:

> Many of our domestic problems are caused on the other side of the world. Financial instability in Asia destroys jobs in Chicago and in my own constituency in County Durham. Poverty in the Caribbean means more drugs on the streets of Washington and London. Conflict in the Balkans causes more refugees in Germany and here in the US. These problems can only be addressed by international co-operation. We are all internationalists now, whether we like it or not. (Blair, 1999)

Definitions of crime begin to change with globalization; while the opportunities for organized, international crime have expanded. Yet, we must ask, do globalization and change bring new questions to criminology or old ones in new outfits?

Global crime

What are the potential consequences of globalization for criminology? As we saw in chapter 7, what we regard as crime and criminal is a complex issue that tends to vary over time and place. However, the whole matter becomes even more complex when we take account of globalization.

Although globalization has broken down many political and financial boundaries, there are still real borders and differences between countries. So what is regarded as a crime in one country may be defined quite differently in another. However, one consequence of globalization is that international laws and agreements are continually being developed by alliances such as the European Union, in order to increase international co-operation and reach some universal consensus about particular issues. Yet what happens when such legislation is at odds with the policy and practice of individual countries?

The UN Convention on the Rights of the Child (United Nations, 1989) came into force in the UK in 1992, although even at the time of ratification the British government was ambiguous in its response to some of the convention's provisions. Currently, the UK government's youth justice policies on locking up juvenile offenders are in breach of this convention. Article 37 of the convention states that children should be detained or imprisoned as a measure of last resort and for the shortest appropriate time. Yet recent youth justice measures in the UK have seen an increasing number of children locked up, and the government has announced plans to build further secure provision for 12–14-year-old offenders (Home Office, 2001).

According to the government, there should be provision to lock up children who have committed crimes. Yet according to the UN convention, children have various needs and rights that are not met in penal settings. So who has committed a crime when a young person is sentenced to prison because of their offending behaviour? The young person for violating the law, or the government for denying them their rights as children? Depending on how we define crime, it is arguable that both parties may be in the wrong.

Organized crime

A further consequence of globalization is that organized crime is changing. According to Interpol – the International Criminal Police Organization – international organized crime is becoming increasingly complex. Ease of travel has made it more possible for criminals to move around the world and link up with new markets. New population movements have also enabled the extension of criminal alliances and networks. Meanwhile, advances in technology and communications have made the planning and commission of international crime much easier, and at the same time more difficult to detect.

Electronic dot-com businesses have been a major growth area, and Internet banking is increasingly used, making the movement of funds and settling of accounts over the Internet vulnerable to exploitation by organized criminals. Credit card fraud and money laundering are particularly difficult to detect, as the offenders could be anywhere in the world (see box 8.2).

Hence, it is clear that the opportunities for certain sorts of crime are changing. Organized crime has always existed, but in the current global climate it looks set to take a more central position on the criminological stage.

Conflict on a global scale has resulted in an increasing number of asylum seekers and displaced persons fleeing from their home countries; consequently the smuggling of illegal immigrants is now a huge industry. News reports telling of large groups of refugees making perilous journeys to more peaceful nations are commonplace, while international responsibility for them is a contentious issue that can itself lead to conflict and disagreement between nations.

In Britain, as in many other western countries, the resources of local authority social services departments are being stretched to deal

---

**BOX 8.2   THE NEW FACE AND CHALLENGES OF
ORGANIZED CRIME**

Cyber crime. Corruption. Money laundering. Arms trafficking. Encryption of criminal communications. Environmental crime. International fraud involving travel documents and credit cards. Crime over the Internet. Theft of art, antiques and cultural property. International terrorism and weapons of mass destruction. Trafficking in body parts. Crimes against women and children. This is a portrait of the changing dimensions and scope of crime facing the international police community today, a criminal industry that takes in an estimated $1,000 billion in illicit profits annually.

The major developments we hold as measures of progress in society, such as split-second communications and transfers of finances anywhere in the world, coupled with the growth and ease of international travel, have also been fully exploited by criminal elements in society. Just as the bi-polar geopolitical world has disintegrated, giving way to a new, dynamic and volatile global environment, the nature of organized crime and criminal extremism/terrorism is evolving as well.

Source: Adapted from Robert C. Fahlman (Assistant Director at Interpol General Secretariat in Lyon, France), 'Intelligence led policing and the key role of criminal intelligence analysis: preparing for the 21st century', www.interpol.com/Public/cia/fahlman.asp#author

---

with the arrival of 'unaccompanied children'. This is a particular problem in London and other inner-city areas, where appropriate welfare resources for children in need are already scarce. In a country where the gap between rich and poor is growing all the time, help offered to asylum seekers inevitably causes resentment among those who live in the most deprived areas and receive little help themselves.

Complaints that local children no longer receive special needs help because the teacher now has to work with the Kosovans may seem justified, but they are a consequence of the overall lack of teaching resources in the education sector. Sadly, the media try to simplify rather then comprehend such links. The academic role is clear: the explanation needs to be sought in the wider structural and cultural constraints that help to fuel such tensions. The important point for the criminologist to grasp is that the painful situation of refugees has the potential to heighten the racial tension that exists in many parts of the country.

Old and new questions

In chapter 5 we outlined some key moments in the history of criminological ideas. The issue of recurring themes was highlighted, and we questioned whether crime theorists already knew all the right questions to ask. At the beginning of the twenty-first century, we believe that there are both old and new questions that criminology must confront.

Not least, academics increasingly use the Internet as a rich resource that provides easy access to vast amounts of knowledge and information from all over the world. Journal articles, conference papers and government reports are frequently published on the worldwide web. The use of e-mail enables split-second communication with colleagues from around the globe.

Curiously, such ease in communication seems to have taken British criminology closer to that of Europe. In chapter 1 we made a plea to 'Remember Europe' in understanding the history of criminology, as many commentators skip straight to developments in Britain and America when outlining where the discipline came from. Some European nations have a long tradition of community measures to control crime. Such measures are a useful antidote to the incapacitation approaches that reflect the American experience, which has taken so much of our attention (as we shall see under 'The future of crime control').

The European Society of Criminology's first ever conference was held in September 2001 and was an opportunity for criminologists from Europe and beyond to share ideas, disseminate knowledge and discuss the use of different national strategies for dealing with crime. Although international criminology conferences are certainly not new, the introduction of a specific annual event in Europe is perhaps a recognition of the fact that Europeans ought to increasingly work with, and learn from, their neighbours. Is this the start of something new or a return to criminological roots?

The age-old Lombrosian question – what is the difference between offenders and non-offenders, 'us' and 'them' – is certainly still being asked, although advances in DNA technology and the development of genetics mean that the answers are generally offered in more sophisticated terms. However, criminologists must not be seduced unthinkingly by this apparent sophistication. It is easy to seek comfort from the belief that criminals are somehow different from the rest of us.

Radical solutions to social problems based on biological explanations have a long history. Ray (1983) has shown how the Eugenics Society was an influential movement in Britain between the wars (between 1918 and 1939). The society's council included such well-known thinkers and writers as John Maynard Keynes, Julian Huxley, William Beveridge (later architect of the post-1945 welfare state), Leonard Darwin and many leading doctors, scientists and sociologists – reflecting the wish to develop a quasi-medical programme that identified the source of social problems as lying beyond social or economic factors. It located the source of pauperism, illness, unemployment – in a word, inequality – in genetic, constitutional or inherited psychological characteristics. Perhaps because the eugenics movement did not have a profound effect in Britain in the way that it did, for example, in Nazi Germany (with the ultimate horrors of the gas chambers), it remains a curiosity that, interestingly, never goes away.

However, the increasingly popular notion of the 'born criminal' – that many thought was buried with the demise of Lombroso – is a pernicious term that confuses the biological and social domains. Being born is a biological fact, while crime is a social construction. Being born is an absolute state, while crime is a relative phenomenon that can vary from society to society. This is an old question dressed up in new and apparently more sophisticated clothes.

By contrast, as a result of globalization and the changing face of international, organized crime, we believe that the criminology of the future will be faced with some new questions. In particular, there will be a concern with how to identify specific offenders in our increasingly interconnected, interdependent world. At present it is relatively easy for people to slip in and out of countries unnoticed, and crimes over the Internet are incredibly difficult to detect as the offenders could be based anywhere in the world.

Concern over the threats posed by international terrorist organizations took centre stage with the horrific events at the World Trade Centre in New York and the Pentagon in Washington on 11 September 2001. Terrorists represent a very real threat to us all, yet there is a danger that politicians will use this to justify introducing increased powers of surveillance for the state, which may be at the expense of individual civil liberties. The introduction of CCTV all over the UK is one of several factors that has led some to question whether we are moving closer towards a Big Brother state (see Maguire, 1998). At times of crisis government proposals to introduce stronger Internet surveillance laws and reintroduce national identity cards indicate that questions of civil liberties and human rights are likely to be important ones for criminology.

Traditional questions about the impact of the social environment on crime and criminality remain important. However, they now need to be extended to consider the impact of the international environment. International terrorism is being fought with global alliances, a reminder that we have newer versions of crimes committed *against* the physical environment itself: for instance, pollution, the threat of chemical warfare, the aftermath of weapons used in previous engagements such as the Gulf War and Kosovo. International alliances are formed to produce international solutions to national problems, and suspected local war criminals are tried in international courts (such as Milosovic, with a trial in the Netherlands). These are complex matters. At the very least, co-operation between national law enforcement agencies around the world will be an important requirement, particularly in the fight against global terror.

The future of crime control

In an important new study, Garland (2001) documents some key similarities between the politics of law and order in Britain and in the USA. In particular, he argues that a culture of control has grown up in these two countries whereby contemporary criminal justice arrangements have a strongly punitive emphasis. Criminal justice thinking has long been characterized by a tension between punishment and welfare. The question of how far we should try to help offenders, in order to prevent them from offending again, is a contentious one. However, Garland's analysis suggests that the current emphasis swings firmly towards punishment and control, and so towards *anti-welfare* politics.

Although the move away from welfare represents a complete shift from criminal justice thinking prior to 1970, Garland argues that we have quickly become used to such arrangements. The culture of control is now taken for granted:

In the USA the public now seems quite accustomed to living in a nation that holds two million of its citizens in confinement on any given day, and puts criminal offenders to death at a rate of two or more per week. In much the same way, the British public no longer seems surprised by the existence of private prisons that house an increasing proportion of Britain's prisoners, and citizens go about their business hardly noticing the surveillance cameras that stare down on the streets of every major city. (Garland, 2001: 1)

According to Garland, the new culture of control has emerged in response to social and economic changes. As we discussed earlier in the context of globalization, we are indeed living in a changing world. However, one consequence of this that has not been considered so far is the uncertainty and insecurity that changing times may bring.

In Garland's view, contemporary British and American societies are characterized by insecurity and an increasing fear of crime; many people see themselves as potential victims. High crime rates are regarded as normal; private, defensive routines are widespread; crime issues are regularly represented in emotive terms; and concerns about public safety dominate public policy. These are just some aspects of what Garland describes as 'the "crime complex" of late modernity' (2001: 163).

The 'crime complex' fuels a desire to manage crime and reduce potential risks to the public. Against this backdrop, increased security, surveillance and control become an inevitable part of the social landscape. The danger is that the heightened fear of crime that is characteristic of the 'crime complex' may in fact obscure the reality of contemporary crime rates.

As Garland comments, although crime rates fell steadily in both the UK and the USA during most of the 1990s, there were at the same time unprecedented rises in imprisonment rates in both countries. While Britain is not in quite the same league as the USA, being slightly less eager to use prison as an option, its own prison population is undoubtedly growing rapidly.

So what does all this mean for criminology? As Garland notes, the future is not inevitable. However, if current trends in crime control continue, there will almost certainly be a duty upon criminologists to provide the voice of reason in a society in which crime issues are usually discussed in emotive terms.

Even in the current crime–control climate, an important role for criminology is to encourage rational and reasoned debate about how to deal humanely and effectively with offenders.

Policies that punish and exclude offenders may well ease public fears in the short term – while conveniently deflecting attention from the structural causes of crime – but they are certainly not a desirable long-term solution to maintaining social order. The crucial point is that, unless the structural causes of crime are brought into focus, then more and more people will be deemed to be suitable for exclusion. One example: when a local drug baron is removed from his sphere of activity, the drug problem does not go away. Instead, in a remarkably short time, a replacement drug baron emerges, probably appreciative of the market opportunity created by the removal of a competitor. Hence, removing known criminals does not necessarily also remove the crime problem.

Using the criminal law as a form of social control

We need to recognize that there are considerable dangers if we rely upon a criminal solution to all social problems and if we criminalize situations that need not concern the criminal justice system. As Garland argues, tough crime policies are not without their costs: 'New powers for police, higher sentencing levels, restrictions on the freedom of ex-offenders – each of these carries a price in terms of the erosion of civil liberties and the reduced power of the citizen *vis-à-vis* the state' (2001: 146).

One should not just accept the status quo, that is, accept what is the current legal system. Criminologists need to ask themselves, for example, if there has been over-legislation in the area of deviance (i.e. sexual behaviour, vice and so on). While, on the one hand, there is a danger of unnecessary criminalization, there is equally a need to ask whether there has been a failure to criminalize other activities sufficiently – perhaps activities that tend to favour certain dominant interests in society but are detrimental to the health and environment of the general community. So, for example, pollution into rivers does not seem to arouse the same interest and excitement as the concern over the years about smoking marijuana.

Criminologists perhaps need to ask more often 'why criminalize?' At rock bottom, criminalizing activity represents failure. It means that other mechanisms of social control have failed – that people harm others or engage in activities that the rest of society abhor. Over-criminalization tends to suggest that the criminal law is being used as a control in areas or activities that people may not like but that are not necessarily harmful. By contrast, a plea about the *failure* to criminalize may point to areas or activities where harm is being enacted but the sanction of the criminal law is either not available or is not being used.

Ultimately the criminal law is an *external* force (sanctioned by the state) to curb proscribed activity. It operates when *internal* controls, normally referred to as conscience, have failed. In past times, religion had a powerful influence in building up this element of self-control. People did not do things because they felt they were morally wrong actions; if, on occasion, they did, they would say they had a 'guilty conscience'. Thus religion has been a powerful force for social control – famously described by Marx (1843–4: 131) as 'the opium of the people'. Religion had a beneficent impact when it helped people to behave with consideration towards each other; it had a maleficent impact when it proscribed activity that was not harmful but was enjoyable. The search to find a unifying moral code, which we all share in a diverse, multicultural and relatively fragmented society, is, of necessity, exclusionary. So, more recently, politicians of various political parties have appealed to the notion of 'family values' as the most appropriate vehicle for learning how to behave appropriately in society and how to restrain individual excesses of behaviour. This presents a limited view of society's demographic structure. It also fails to reflect the reality of a world in which images from the media as well as traditional peer group pressures have a tremendous impact on individuals and their worldview.

Conformity is both a danger and a delight. It is a danger when everyone conforms because it suggests that the external controls are so strong that everyone is too scared to deviate – powerfully portrayed in some of George Orwell's famous novels, most notably *1984*. This has occurred in totalitarian states when everyone is a potential spy on his or her neighbour (see, for example, Garton Ash's 1997 account of discovering who among his East Berlin acquaintances contributed to his Stasi file, which he read after the fall of the Berlin Wall). Conformity can also, however, be a delight when everyone at the end of a bank holiday either deposits their rubbish in bins or takes it home with them. It is salutary to consider how much the force of the criminal law can contribute to the fulfilment of the latter. The Litter Act 1983 has perhaps the symbolic function of declaring that leaving litter is regarded as inappropriate behaviour, but seems to have little or no impact on the pervasiveness (or otherwise) of the behaviour.

Two examples from motoring behaviour show how internal and external controls seem to work rather differently. The careful and well-orchestrated introduction of seat-belt legislation has been a remarkable success. The vast majority of motorists in the United Kingdom nowadays 'belt up' and, while there is a law on the statute book, it rarely needs to be enforced. Motorists have the self-control to take the appropriate action without being consistently reminded of the threat of a penal sanction. In contrast, speeding, with the widespread introduction of CCTV cameras as a technological back-up to police vigilance, is largely being kept in check by the threat of external controls. Why are we willing to 'belt up' without the persistent intervention of the police or their technological handmaidens, and yet unwilling to slow down without consistent surveillance? An introduction to criminology is not going to produce an easy answer to this fascinating dilemma or even try to probe a more difficult answer. However, we will identify as a crucial issue for criminologists the gulf between responses to laws which become internalized 'values' within individuals and those which are only enforced by external powers.

Our perceptions of crime, detection and policing are shaped, as we saw in chapter 2, by fiction, film and television. Definitions of the 'crime problem' and, hence, criminology itself are increasingly media-led. There is a steady diet of homicide and serial killing on television and at the cinema, which makes the discipline of criminology sound exciting and stimulating while making the world appear a fearful place. However, such events, although still very important, are only the tip of the iceberg we call criminology. There are more profound and significant issues to confront – not least, the quality of life for the bulk of people, their fears, their safety and their belief in justice to protect them and those closest to them. Criminologists need to decide whether the most mundane questions of how and why we behave are issues to consider, or whether the talents of a new generation of criminologists should simply focus on a narrow set of issues bounded by murder at the peak and juvenile delinquency at the base.

In this chapter we have tried to do two things to widen the current scope of criminology. First, we have emphasized the impact of change, particularly globalization. However, we have also asked if recent packaging perhaps only masks some very old and familiar problems. It is misleading to argue that *all* contemporary problems are simply variants of old issues. So, for example, the impact of the motor car on crime at the beginning of the twentieth century was limited, but fifty years later perhaps half of all offenders were being charged for motoring offences. Perhaps in the twenty-first century this will be matched by the impact of the Internet on crime.

Second, we have suggested that the questions of criminology are at the very heart of questions about social order. Hence, the discourse of criminology encourages one to step back and consider the wider political and social matters that surround crime and criminality, punishment and offending, deviance and conformity. These are all central topics in the debate about how and why societies choose the solutions they do to questions of social order. Thus, by building on and borrowing from related but separate disciplines, the debate is rich and complex. Not all commentators on crime would call themselves criminologists, but nonetheless their insights add new dimensions to the discourse of criminology. Therefore, as scholars, you need to recognize that criminology is not a narrow discipline, and to come to an understanding of most criminological issues you will need to appreciate the work of many other disciplines.

More important, as citizens, you need to recognize the dangers of over-criminalizing society. The development of criminology has many links with the failure of all of us to develop society in a way that eliminates both greed and need. Criminology has a symbiotic relationship with the criminal law. Criminologists should be at the front line as informed citizens, able to identify the dangers of criminalizing dissent, on the one hand, and of letting the powerful off the hook, on the other.

Resources for Further Study

FURTHER READING

Chapter 1

Giddens, A., *Sociology* (3rd edn) (Cambridge: Polity, 1997). (See chapter 8 on 'Deviance and crime').

Soothill, K., 'Deviance, crime and control'. In Abercrombie, N., Warde, A., Deem, R., Penna, S., Soothill, K., Urry, J., Sayer, A. and Walby, S. *Contemporary British Society* (3rd edn) (Cambridge: Polity, 2000), pp. 513–48.

Chapter 2

Coleman, C. and Moynihan, J., *Understanding Crime Data: Haunted by the Dark Figure* (Buckingham: Open University Press, 1996).

Mirlees-Black, C., Budd, T., Partridge, S. and Mayhew, P., 'The 1998 British Crime Survey: England and Wales', *Home Office Statistical Bulletin 21/98* (London: Home Office, 1998).

Chapter 3

Cavadino, M. and Dignan, J., *The Penal System: An Introduction* (3rd edn), (London: Sage, 2001).

Davies, M., Croall, H. and Tyrer, J., *Criminal Justice: An Introduction to the Criminal Justice System in England and Wales* (2nd edn) (Essex: Longman, 1998).

Chapter 4

Clancy, A., Hough, M., Aust, R. and Kershaw, C., 'Crime, policing and justice: the experience of ethnic minorities. Findings from the 2000 British

Crime Survey', *Home Office Research Study 223* (London: Home Office, 2001).

Walklate, S., *Gender, Crime and Criminal Justice* (Devon: Willan, 2001).

Chapter 5

Lilly, J. R., Cullen, F. T. and Ball R. A., *Criminological Theory: Context and Consequences* (3rd edn) (London: Sage, 2001).

Becker, H. S., *Outsiders* (New York: Free Press, 1963, 1997).

Chapter 6

Alcock, C., Payne, S. and Sullivan, M., *Introducing Social Policy* (Essex: Pearson Education Ltd, 2000).

Muncie, J., *Youth and Crime: A Critical Introduction* (London: Sage, 1999).

Chapter 7

Cohen, S., *States of Denial: Knowing about Atrocities and Suffering* (Cambridge: Polity, 2001).

Croall, H. and Maguire, M., *Understanding White Collar Crime* (Buckingham: Open University Press, 2001).

Chapter 8

Fattah, E., *Criminology: Past, Present and Future: A Critical Overview* (London: Macmillan, 1997).

Garland, D. (ed.), *Mass Imprisonment: Social Causes and Consequences* (London: Sage, 2001).

GENERAL READING

McLaughlin, E. and Muncie, J. (eds), *The Sage Dictionary of Criminology* (London: Sage, 2001).

Maguire, M., Morgan, R. and Reiner, R. (eds), *The Oxford Handbook of Criminology* (3rd edn) (Oxford: Oxford University Press, 2002).

JOURNALS

The journals below are all published quarterly, apart from the *Howard Journal* which is now published five times a year. As journals are published relatively frequently, the articles that they contain provide readers with some of the most up-to-date material in criminology.

American Journal of Criminology   The official publication of the American Society of Criminology.

British Journal of Criminology   The official publication of the British Society of Criminology.

Howard Journal of Criminal Justice   Published by the Howard League of Penal Reform. This journal focuses particularly on criminal justice issues.

Theoretical Criminology   An international journal concerned with theoretical debates and advancing theoretical aspects of criminology.

SOME USEFUL WEBSITES

Home Office   http://www.homeoffice.gov.uk
The official government department that is responsible for internal affairs in England and Wales. The Home Office deals with a variety of crime-related issues.

Nacro (The National Association for the Care and Resettlement of Offenders)   http://www.nacro.org.uk
Nacro is an independent voluntary organization working to prevent crime.

Howard League for Penal Reform   http://www.howardleague.org
An independent organization working for the humane reform of the penal system.

Liberty   http://www.liberty-human-rights.org.uk
An independent human rights organization which works to defend and extend rights and freedoms in England and Wales.

Interpol   http://www.interpol.com
The International Criminal Police Organization.

Bibliography

Abercrombie, N. and Warde, A. with Deem, R., Penna, S., Soothill, K., Urry, J., Sayer, A. and Walby, S. (2000) *Contemporary British Society* (3rd edn). Cambridge: Polity.

Agnew, R. (1992) 'Foundation for a general strain theory of crime and delinquency'. *Criminology*, 30, 47–66.

Anderson, S., Kinsey, R., Loader, I. and Smith, C. (1994) *Cautionary Tales: Young People, Crime and Policing in Edinburgh*. Aldershot: Avebury.

Aye Maung, N. (1995) *Young People, Victimisation and the Police: British Crime Survey Findings on Experiences and Attitudes of 12 to 15 year olds*. London: HMSO.

Baldwin, J. (1985) 'Pre-trial settlement in the magistrates' courts'. *Howard Journal of Criminal Justice*, 24 (2), 108–17.

Baldwin, J. and McConville, M. (1977) *Negotiated Justice*. Oxford: Blackwell.

Barclay, G. and Mhlanga, B. (2000) *Ethnic Differences in Decisions on Young Defendants Dealt with by the Crown Prosecution Service*, Section 95 Findings, No. 1. London: Home Office.

Becker, H. (1963) *Outsiders*. New York: The Free Press.

Becker, H. (1967) 'Whose side are we on?'. *Social Problems*, 14, 239–247.

Behr, E. (1997) *Prohibition: The 13 Years that Changed America*. BBC: London.

Blair, T. (1999) Speech to the Economic Club of Chicago, USA (22 April 1999). www.fco.gov.uk/news/speechtext.asp?2316.

Blake, M. (1997) *As If*. London: Granta.

Blumstein, A., Cohen, J., Roth, J. A. and Visher, C. A. (1986) *Criminal Careers and 'Career Criminals'* (vol. 1). Washington DC: National Academy Press.

Booth, T. (1988) *Developing Policy Research*. Aldershot: Avebury.

Bowden, M. (2001) *Killing Pablo: The Hunt for the Richest, Most Powerful Criminal in History*. London: Atlantic Press.

Bower, T. (1991) *Maxwell: The Outsider* (2nd edn). London: Heinemann.

Box, S. (1971) *Deviance, Reality and Society*. London: Holt, Rinehart & Winston.

Box, S. (1981) *Deviance, Reality and Society* (2nd edn). London: Holt, Rinehart & Winston.

Box, S. (1983) *Power, Crime and Mystification*. London: Tavistock.

Braithwaite, J. (1989) *Crime, Shame and Reintegration*. Cambridge: Cambridge University Press.

Broad, B. (1998) *Young People Leaving Care: Life After the Children Act 1989*. London: Jessica Kingsley.

Burgess, E. W. (1925) 'The growth of the city'. In R. E. Park, E. W. Burgess and R. D. McKenzie (eds), *The City*, Chicago: University of Chicago Press, pp. 47–62.

Burt, C. (1925) *The Young Delinquent*. London: University of London Press.

Butler, R. (1974) 'The foundation of the Institute of Criminology in Cambridge'. In R. Hood (ed.), *Crime, Criminology and Public Policy: Essays in Honour of Sir Leon Radzinowicz*, London: Heinemann, pp. 1–10.

Carlen, P. (1985) *Criminal Women*. Cambridge: Polity.

Chambliss, W. B. (1975) 'Toward a political economy of crime'. *Theory and Society*, 2, 152–3.

Chambliss, W. (2000) 'High points and low points in twentieth century criminology'. Paper given in presidential plenary at the American Society of Criminology's 52nd annual meeting, November 15–18, San Francisco, California.

Children and Young Persons Unit (2001) *Tomorrow's Future: Building a Strategy for Children and Young People*. London: Children and Young Person's Unit.

Clarke, J. and Critcher, C. (1985) *The Devil Makes Work: Leisure in Capitalist Britain*. Basingstoke: Macmillan.

Cohen, A. K. (1955) *Delinquent Boys: The Culture of the Gang*. New York: Free Press.

Cohen, S. (ed.) (1971) *Images of Deviance*. Harmondsworth: Penguin.

Cohen, S. (1971) 'Introduction'. In S. Cohen (ed.), *Images of Deviance*, Harmondsworth: Penguin, pp. 9–25.

Cohen, S. (1973) *Folk Devils and Moral Panics*. London: Paladin.

Cohen, S. (1985) *Visions of Social Control*. Cambridge: Polity.

Cohen, S. (1985) 'Criminology'. In A. Kuper and J. Kuper (eds), *The Social Science Encyclopaedia*, London: Routledge, pp. 173–5.

Cohen, S. (1988) *Against Criminology*. New Brunswick NJ: Transaction.

Cohen, S. (2001) *States of Denial: Knowing About Atrocities and Suffering*. Cambridge: Polity.

Cohen, S. and Taylor, L. (1972) *Psychological Survival: The Experience of Long-term Imprisonment*. Harmondsworth: Penguin.

Daly, M. (1979) *Gyn/Ecology*. London: Women's Press.

Defoe, D. (1996) *Moll Flanders* (first published 1722). London: Penguin.

Denman, S. (2001) 'Race discrimination in the Crown Prosecution Service'. www.cps.gov.uk/cps_a/denman.pdf.

Dobson, R. (2000) 'Childhood betrayed', *Independent on Sunday*, 20 February, p. 16.

Downes, D. (1988) 'The sociology of crime and social control in Britain, 1960–1987'. *British Journal of Criminology*, 28, 175–87.

Downes, D. (1997) 'Dumping the "hostages to fortune"? the politics of law and order in post-war Britain'. In M. Maguire, M. Morgan and R. Reiner (eds), *The Oxford Handbook of Criminology*, Oxford: Oxford University Press, pp. 87–134.

Downes, D. and Rock, P. (1998) *Understanding Deviance: A Guide to the Sociology of Crime and Law-breaking* (3rd edn). Oxford: Oxford University Press.

Dyer, C. (1999) 'Law', *Guardian*, 19 June.

East, K. and Campbell, S. (2001) 'Aspects of crime: young offenders 1999'. Home Office (Internet only). www.homeoffice.gov.uk/rds/pdfs/aspects-youngoffs.pdf.

Eaton, M. (1986) *Justice for Women? Family, Court and Social Control*. Milton Keynes: Open University Press.

Erikson, K. T. (1964) 'Notes on the sociology of deviance'. In H. S. Becker (ed.), *The Other Side: Perspectives on Deviance*, New York: The Free Press, pp. 9–21.

Fahlman, R. C. (1999) 'Intelligence-led policing and the key role of criminal intelligence analysis: preparing for the 21st century'. www.interpol.com/Public/cia/fahlman.asp#author.

Farrington, D. P. (1989) 'Self-reported and official offending from adolescence to adulthood'. In M. W. Klein (ed.), *Cross-National Research in Self-reported Crime and Delinquency*, Dordrecht: Kluwer, pp. 339–423.

Farrington, D. (1992) 'Criminal career research in the United Kingdom'. *British Journal of Criminology*, 32, 521–36.

Farrington, D. (1995) 'The development of offending and antisocial behaviour from childhood: key findings from the Cambridge Study in Delinquent Development'. *Journal of Child Psychology and Psychiatry*, 36, 929–64.

Finch, J. (1986) *Research and Policy*. East Sussex: The Falmer Press.

Fitzgerald, M. and Sibbitt, R. (1997) 'Ethnic monitoring in police forces: a beginning'. In *Home Office Research Study 173*, London: Home Office.

Flood-Page, C., Campbell, S., Harrington, V. and Miller, J. (2000) 'Youth crime: findings from the 1998/99 Youth Lifestyles Survey'. Home Office Research Study 209, London: Home Office.

Foster, J. (1990) *Villains: Crime and Community in the Inner City*. London: Routledge.

Garland, D. (1997) 'Of crimes and criminals: The development of criminology in Britain'. In M. Maguire, R. Morgan and R. Reiner (eds), *The Oxford Handbook of Criminology* (2nd edn), Oxford: Oxford University Press.

Garland, D. (2001) *The Culture of Control: Crime and Social Order in Contemporary Society*. Oxford: Oxford University Press.

Garland, D. and Sparks, R. (2000) 'Criminology, social theory and the challenge of our times'. In D. Garland and R. Sparks (eds), *Criminology and Social Theory*, Oxford: Oxford University Press.

Garton Ash, T. (1997) *The File: A Personal History*. London: Flamingo/ Harper Collins.

Gelsthorpe, L. and Morris, A. (eds) (1990) *Feminist Perspectives in Criminology*. Buckingham: Open University Press.

Goffman, E. (1968a) *Asylums: Essays on the Social Situation of Mental Patients and Other Inmates*. Harmondsworth: Penguin.

Goffman, E. (1968b) *Stigma: Notes on the Management of Spoiled Identity*. Harmondsworth: Penguin.

Goldson, B. and Peters, E. (2000) *Tough Justice: Responding to Children in Trouble*. London: The Children's Society.

Goring, C. (1913) *The English Convict: A Statistical Study*. London: HMSO.

Gottfredson, M. R. and Hirschi, T. (1990) *A General Theory of Crime*. Stanford CA: Stanford University Press.

Gottlieb, A. (2000) 'Socrates: Philosophy's martyr'. In F. Raphael and R. Monk (eds), *The Great Philosophers*, London: Weidenfeld & Nicholoson.

Greenleaf, History of the troubles: the battles for Stonehenge. www.greenleaf.demon.co.uk/h850601.htm.

Gryn, H. with N. (2001) *Chasing Shadows*. London: Penguin.

Guedalla, P. (1920) from *Supers and Supermen*. Quoted in *The Oxford Dictionary of Quotations* (1992; 4th edn), Oxford: Oxford University Press, p. 319.

Hagan, J. (1994) *Crime and Disrepute*. Thousand Oaks CA: Pine Forge Press.

Hall, S. and Scraton, P. (1981) 'Law, class and control'. In M. Fitzgerald, G. McLennan and J. Pawson (eds), *Crime and Society: Readings in History and Theory*, London: Routledge & Kegan Paul.

Haste, C. (1992) *Rules of Desire: Sex in Britain: World War I to the Present*. London: Chatto & Windus.

Heidensohn, F. (2000) *Sexual Politics and Social Control*. Buckingham: Open University Press.

Hirschi, T. (1969) *Causes of Delinquency*. Berkeley CA: University of California Press.

Hirschi, T. (1979) 'Separate and unequal is better'. *Journal of Research in Crime and Delinquency*, 16, 34–8.

Home Affairs Committee (1984) *Compensation and Support for Victims of Crime and Minutes of Evidence*. London: HMSO.

Home Office (2000a) *Statistics on Race and the Criminal Justice System*. Section 95 Criminal Justice Act publication, London: Home Office.

Home Office (2000b) *Statistics on Women and the Criminal Justice System*. Section 95 Criminal Justice Act publication, London: Home Office.

Home Office (2001) *Criminal Justice: The Way Ahead*. Cm 5074. London: HMSO.

Hough, M. and Mayhew, P. (1985) 'Taking account of crime: key findings from the 1984 British Crime Survey'. In *Home Office Research Study No. 85*, London: HMSO.

Human Rights Watch (1999) 'Leave none to tell the story: genocide in Rwanda'. www.hrw.org/reports/1999/rwanda/GenO15-8-05.htm.

Hylton, S. (2001) *Their Darkest Hour: The Hidden History of the Home Front 1939–1945*. Stroud, Glos: Sutton.

Jeffrey, C. R. (1960) 'The historical development of criminology'. In H. Mannheim (ed.), *Pioneers of Criminology*, Chicago: Quadrangle, pp. 364–94.

Jones, G. and Bell, R. (2000) *Balancing Acts: Youth, Parenting and Public Policy*. York: York Publishing Services / Joseph Rowntree Foundation.

Jones, S. (1996) 'The criminal gene', *Daily Telegraph*, 27 April.

Jones, T., Maclean, B. and Young, J. (1986) *The Islington Crime Survey*. London: Gower.

Kilsby, P. (2001) 'Aspects of crime: children as victims 1999'. Home Office (Internet only). www.homeoffice.gov.uk/rds/pdfs/aspects-children.pdf.

Kitsuse, J. I. and Cicourel, A. V. (1963) 'A note on the uses of official statistics'. *Social Problems*, 2, 131–9.

Kohn, M. (1992) *Dope Girls: The Birth of the British Drug Underground*. London: Granta books.

Kuhn, T. S. (1962) *The Structure of Scientific Revolutions*. Chicago: University of Chicago Press.

Lacey, N. (1994) 'Missing the wood . . . pragmatism versus theory in the royal commission'. In M. McConville and L. Bridges (eds), *Criminal Justice in Crisis*, Aldershot: Edward Elgar, pp. 30–41.

Laing, R. D. and Esterson, A. (1973) *Sanity, Madness and the Family* (2nd edn). Harmondsworth: Penguin.

Lemert, E. M. (1967) *Human Deviance, Social Problems and Social Control*. New Jersey: Prentice-Hall.

Liebrich, J. (1993) *Straight To The Point: Angles on Giving up Crime*. Wellington, New Zealand: University of Otago Press.

Lipton, P. (2001) 'Kant on wheels'. *London Review of Books*, 23 (14), 30–1.

Lombroso, C. (1876) *L'Uomo delinquente*. Turin: Fratelli Bocca.

Luttwak, E. (2001) 'Napoleon of Medellin'. *London Review of Books*, 23 (19), 15–16.

McLevy, J. (1975) *The Casebook of a Victorian Detective*. Edinburgh: Canongate.

Maguire, M. (1982) *Burglary in a Dwelling*. London: Heinemann.

Maguire, M. (1998) 'Restraining Big Brother? The regulation of surveillance in England and Wales'. In C. Norris, J. Moran and G. Armstrong (eds), *Surveillance, Closed Circuit Television and Social Control*, Aldershot: Ashgate, pp. 229–40.

Maguire, M. and Corbett, C. (1987) *The Effects of Crime and the Work of Victim Support Schemes*. Aldershot: Gower.

Mannheim, H. (1965) *Comparative Criminology: A Text Book* (2 vols). London: Routledge.

Manning, P. K. (1971) 'The police: mandate, strategies, and appearances'. In J. D. Douglas (ed.), *Crime and Justice in American Society*, Indianapolis: Bobbs-Merrill, pp. 149–93.

Mark, R. (1978) *In the Office of Constable*. London: Collins.

Martin, J. P. (1988) 'The development of criminology in Britain, 1948–60'. *British Journal of Criminology*, 28, 165–74.

Maruna, S. (2001) *Making Good: How Ex-Convicts Reform and Rebuild Their Lives*. Washington DC: American Psychological Association.

Marx, K. (1843–4) 'A contribution to the critique of Hegel's "Philosophy of Right": Introduction'. In J. O'Malley (ed.) *Critique of Hegel's 'Philosophy of Right' by Karl Marx*, London: Cambridge University Press, 1970.

Matthews, R. and Young, J. (1992) 'Reflections on realism'. In J. Young and R. Matthews (eds), *Rethinking Criminology: The Realist Debate*, London: Sage.

Matza, D. (1964) *Delinquency and Drift*. New York: Wiley.

Matza, D. (1969) *Becoming Deviant*. Englewood Cliffs NJ: Prentice Hall.

Merton, R. K. (1938) 'Social structure and anomie'. *American Sociological Review*, 3, 672–82.

Merton, R. K. (1966) 'Social problems and sociological theory'. In R. K. Merton and R. A. Nisbet (eds), *Contemporary Social Problems*, New York: Harcourt, Brace & World Inc.

Mitchell, B. (1990) *Murder and Penal Policy*. Macmillan: London.

Moffitt, T. E. (1993) 'Adolescence-limited and life-course persistent antisocial behaviour: a developmental taxonomy'. *Psychological Review*, 100, 674–701.

Morel, B. A. (1857) *Traité des dégénérescences physiques, intellectuelles et morales de l'espèce humaine*. Paris: Baillière.

Morgan, R. (2000) 'The politics of criminological research'. In R. King and E. Wincup (eds), *Doing Research on Crime and Justice*, Oxford: Oxford University Press.

Morris, T. (1958) *The Criminal Area: A Study in Social Ecology*. London: Routledge & Kegan Paul.

Nelken, D. (1994) 'White-collar crime'. In M. Maguire, R. Morgan and R. Reiner (eds), *The Oxford Handbook of Criminology* (1st edn), Oxford: Clarendon.

Nelken, D. (1997) 'White-collar crime'. In M. Maguire, R. Morgan and R. Reiner (eds), *The Oxford Handbook of Criminology* (2nd edn), Oxford: Clarendon.

Newburn, T. (1997) 'Youth, crime and justice'. In M. Maguire, R. Morgan and R. Reiner (eds), *The Oxford Handbook of Criminology* (2nd edn), Oxford: Clarendon.

Nisbet, R. A. (1966) *The Sociological Tradition*. New York: Basic Books.

Oliver, M. (1998) *Philosophy*. London: Hamlyn.

Packer, H. (1968) *The Limits of the Criminal Sanction*. Stanford CA: Stanford University Press.

Painter, K., Lea, J., Woodhouse, T. and Young, J. (1989) *Hammersmith and Fulham Crime and Police Survey, 1988*. Middlesex: Centre for Criminology, Middlesex Polytechnic.

Parker, H., Aldridge, J. and Measham, F. (1998) *Illegal Leisure: The Normalization of Adolescent Recreational Drug Use*. London: Routledge.

Pearson, G. (1983) *Hooligan: A History of Respectable Fears*. London: Macmillan.

Pearson, G. (1994) 'Youth, crime and society'. In M. Maguire, R. Morgan and R. Reiner (eds), *The Oxford Handbook of Criminology*, Oxford: Clarendon Press.

Percy, A. (1998) 'Ethnicity and victimisation: findings from the 1996 British Crime Survey'. *Home Office Statistical Bulletin*, 3 April 1998, London: Research and Statistics Directorate.

Pick, D. (1989) *Faces of Degeneration: A European Disorder. c1848-c1918*. Cambridge: Cambridge University Press.

Piper, C. (1999) 'The Crime and Disorder Act 1998: child and community "safety"'. *Modern Law Review*, 62 (3), 397–408.

Povey, K. (2000) *On the Record – Thematic Inspection Report on Police Crime Recording, the Police National Computer and Phoenix Intelligence System Data Quality*. London: Her Majesty's Inspectorate of Constabulary.

Prime, J., White, S., Liriano, S. and Patel, K. (2001) *Criminal Careers of Those Born Between 1953 and 1978*. London: Home Office Research Bulletin.

Quinney, R. (1977) *Class, State and Crime: On the Theory and Practice of Criminal Justice*. New York: Mckay.

Radzinowicz, L. (1961) *In Search of Criminology*. London: Heinemann.

Rafter, N. H. and Natalizia, E. M. (1981) 'Marxist feminism: implications for criminal justice'. *Crime and Delinquency*, 27, 81–98.

Ray, L. (1983) 'Eugenics, mental deficiency and Fabian socialism between the wars'. *Oxford Review of Education*, 1983.

Rock, P. (1990) *Helping Victims of Crime*. Oxford: Clarendon.

Rock, P. (1995) 'The opening stages of criminal justice policy making'. *British Journal of Criminology*, 35 (1), 1–16.

Rosenberger, A. (2001) *End of the Road: Travellers and the Criminal Justice Bill. Violations of Rights in Britain*, Series 2, No. 16. London: Charter 88. www.charter88.org.uk/pubs/violations/rosen.html.

Sampson, R. and Laub, J. (1993) *Crime in the Making: Pathways and Turning Points Through Life*. London: Harvard University Press.

Scarman, Lord (1981) *The Brixton Disorders 10–12 April 1981: Report of an Inquiry by the Rt. Hon. Lord Scarman, OBE*. Cm. 8427. London: HMSO.

Scott-Moncrieff, G. (1975) 'Foreword'. In J. McLevy, *The Casebook of a Victorian Detective*, Edinburgh: Canongate.

Scraton, P. (1987) 'Unreasonable force: policing, punishment and marginalization'. In P. Scraton (ed.), *Law, Order and the Authoritarian State*, Milton Keynes: Open University Press, pp. 460–97.

Sereny, G. (1998) *Cries Unheard: The Story of Mary Bell*. London: Papermac.

Shapland, J. (1982) 'Compensation and support for victims of violent crime'. Final Report to the Home Office, December 1982. Summary of report at Appendix B of Home Affairs Committee (1984) *Compensation and Support for Victims of Crime and Minutes of Evidence*. London: HMSO.

Shapland, J., Willmore, J. and Duff, P. (1985) *Victims in the Criminal Justice System*. Aldershot: Gower.

Shaw, C. and McKay, H. (1942) *Juvenile Delinquency and Urban Areas*. Chicago: University of Chicago Press.

Sherrin, N. (1996) *The Oxford Dictionary of Humorous Quotations*. Oxford: Oxford University Press.

Sim, J., Scraton, P. and Gordon, P. (1987) 'Introduction: crime, state and critical analysis'. In P. Scraton (ed.), *Law, Order and the Authoritarian State*, Milton Keynes: Open University Press.

Skolnick, J. H. (1966) *Justice without Trial: Law Enforcement in a Democratic Society*. New York: John Wiley & Sons.

Smart, C. (1977) *Women, Crime and Criminology*. London: Routledge & Kegan Paul.

Smith, D. J. (2001) 'Blind justice hits the target: race, crime and policing in England'. Presentation at the first meeting of the European Society of Criminology, Lausanne, Switzerland, 6–8 September.

Social Exclusion Unit (1998) *Bringing Britain Together: A National Strategy for Neighbourhood Renewal*. Cm 4045. London: The Stationery Office.

Social Exclusion Unit (2001) *Preventing Social Exclusion*. www.cabinet-office.gov.uk/seu/2001/pse/PSE%20HTML/default.htm.

Soothill, K. (ed.) (1999) *Criminal Conversations: An Anthology of the Work of Tony Parker*. London: Routledge.

Soothill, K. and Francis, B. (2002) 'Exploring the relationship between homicide and levels of violence in Great Britain'. *Security Journal*, 15 (3), 37–46.

Soothill, K., Adserballe, H., Bernheim, J., Dasamanjali, T., Harding, T. W., Ribeiro, R. P., Reinhold, F. and Soueif, M. I. (1981) 'Social control of deviants in six countries'. *Medicine, Science and the Law*, 21 (1), 31–40.

Soothill, K., Francis, B., Ackerley, E. and Collett, S. (1999) *Homicide in Britain: A Comparative Study of Rates in Scotland and England and Wales*. Edinburgh: Scottish Executive.

Sutherland, E. (1961) *White Collar Crime*. New York: Holt.

Szasz, T. S. (1961) *The Myth of Mental Illness*. New York: Hoeber-Harper.

Tappan, P. W. (1947) 'Who is the criminal?'. *American Sociological Review*, 12, 96–102.

Tash, Stonehenge and 'The battle of the beanfield'. www.gn.apc.org/tash/contents.htm.

Tatar, M. (1995) *Lustmord: Sexual Murder in Weimar Germany*. Princeton NJ: Princeton University Press.

Taylor, C. (2001) 'The relationship between social and self-control: tracing Hirschi's criminological career'. *Theoretical Criminology*, 5 (3), 369–88.

Taylor, I. and Taylor, L. (eds) (1973) *Politics and Deviance*. Harmondsworth: Penguin.

Taylor, I., Walton, P. and Young, J. (1973) *The New Criminology*. London: Routledge & Kegan Paul.

Taylor, I., Walton, P. and Young, J. (eds) (1975) *Critical Criminology*. London: Routledge & Kegan Paul.

Thatcher, M. (1993) *The Downing Street Years*. London: HarperCollins.

Thompson, E. P. (1967) 'Time, work-discipline and industrial capitalism'. *Past and Present*, 38, 56–97.

Thompson, K. (1998) *Moral Panics*. London: Routledge.

Thorpe, D., Smith, D., Green, C. J. and Paley, J. H. (1980) *Out of Care*. London: George Allen and Unwin.

Trevelyan, G. M. (1964) *Illustrated English Social History: Volume 1*. Harmondsworth: Penguin.

United Nations (1989) *The United Nations Convention on the Rights of the Child*. New York: United Nations.

Utting, W. (1999) 'Battles lost or won?'. In B. Holman, R. Parker and W. Utting, *Reshaping Child Care Practice*, London: National Institute for Social Work.

Walker, N. (1991) *Why Punish? Theories of Punishment Reassessed*. Oxford: Oxford University Press.

Walklate, S. (1998) *Understanding Criminology: Current Theoretical Debates*. Buckingham: Open University Press.

Walklate, S. (2001) *Gender, Crime and Criminal Justice*. Cullompton, Devon: Willan.

Warner Brothers (1950) *The Blue Lamp*. Ealing Studios.

Waterhouse, R. (2000) *Lost in Care: Report of the Tribunal of Inquiry into the Abuse of Children in Care in the Former County Council Areas of Gwynedd and Clwyd since 1974*. London: HMSO.

Weber, M. (1968) *Economy and Society*. New York: Free Press.

West, D. J. (1969) *Present Conduct and Future Delinquency*. London: Heinemann.

West, D. J. (1982) *Delinquency: Its Roots, Careers and Prospects*. London: Heinemann.

West, D. J. and Farrington, D. P. (1973) *Who Becomes Delinquent?* London: Heinemann.

West, D. J. and Farrington, D. P. (1977) *The Delinquent Way of Life*. London: Heinemann.

Whyte, W. F. (1955) *Street Corner Society* (2nd edn). Chicago: University of Chicago Press.

Windlesham, Lord (1993) *Responses to Crime, Volume 2: Penal Policy in the Making*. Oxford: Clarendon.

Wright, G. (1983) *Between the Guillotine and Liberty: Two Centuries of the Crime Problem in France*. Oxford: Oxford University Press.

Young, J. (1986) 'The failure of criminology: the need for a radical realism'. In R. Matthews and J. Young (eds), *Confronting Crime*, London: Sage.

Young, J. (1991) *Ten Principles of Realism*. Paper presented at the British Criminology Conference, York.

Young, J. (1992) 'Ten points of realism'. In J. Young and R. Matthews (eds), *Rethinking Criminology: The Realist Debate*, London: Sage.

Zedner, L. (1997) 'Victims'. In M. Maguire, R. Morgan and R. Reiner (eds), *The Oxford Handbook of Criminology* (2nd edn), Oxford: Oxford University Press.

Index